BOWLS:

How to Become a Champion

BOWLS:

How to Become a Champion

C. M. JONES

FABER AND FABER
3 Queen Square
London

First published in 1972
by Faber and Faber Limited
3 Queen Square, London WC1
Printed in Great Britain by
·Latimer Trend & Co Ltd Plymouth
All rights reserved

ISBN 0 571 09859 2

Contents

Introduction   *page* 9

1. Understanding the Green and Your Bowls   11

2. Grip and Delivery   28

3. Fit for Bowls   48

4. How Practice Makes Perfect   67

5. Sighting   82

6. The Seven Shots   93

7. The Different Games   101

8. Their Greatest Ends   104

9. Lessons of the 1970 Commonwealth
   Games   131

10. Personality and Champions   136

11. How Champions Win   145

Bibliography   160

Contents

Illustrations

Complete delivery by Norman King   *facing page* 32

The start of David Bryant's delivery   33

David Bryant in action   33

Delivery by Peter Line   128

Delivery by Percy Baker   128

A winning shot by George Warman   129

Arthur Knowling at the Crystal Palace   129

Introduction

The invention of the ball has been attributed to the Lydians in the reign of Atys. It has been written that Anagalla, a native of Corcyra, presented a ball to Nausicaa, the daughter of King Alcinous of Phaecia, and that she and her handmaidens played with it on the shores of Phaecia.

Pliny, Ovid and others prove that ball games were popular pastimes in the classic ages. Sir Flinders Petrie, the eminent Egyptologist, discovered implements for playing a game similar to modern bowls while examining the contents of the grave of an Egyptian child whose burial was authoritatively placed at 5,200 B.C.

A primitive form of bowls, then, existed in far off times but the unique feature of bowls as we know it is bias. This is the factor which causes a bowl to run a curved path instead of in a straight line, so enabling it to avoid obstacles while finding its way to a target.

The introduction of bias is sometimes credited to Charles Brandon, Duke of Suffolk, during a game played at Goole in the sixteenth century. His bowl having been shattered, he ran indoors in search of another and his eyes fell on the ornamental sphere at the foot of the banisters. Calling for a saw, he cut it free and returned to the garden to continue the game.

The improvised bowl soon showed a novel and challenging characteristic: the slight flattening of the surface where the cut had been made had set up an imbalance which caused a curving run. With this to help him he soon began scoring against heads which, hitherto, had been 'impossible'.

However, bowls with bias have been dug up which appear to pre-date Brandon's game. So a wonderful new game was born. Shakespeare makes Queen Isobel allude to bias in a bowling sense in Act III, scene 4 of *Richard II*.

Enough. Let us pause to pay grateful homage to the benefactor who was actually responsible because it is bias which makes bowls the most skilful ball game on earth.

It is the object of this book to explain the theoretical science of the game and, through detailed study and analysis of the world's greatest players, to provide each reader with the basic knowledge of the way to become a champion.

Whether or not he succeeds will depend on him, for forty-four years of playing, teaching and writing about ball games at top world class levels have convinced me that advanced knowledge cannot be *taught*.

The teacher must be a fountain of knowledge but the pupil must be willing and eager to drink from that fountain; in other words, he must *learn*. The initiative and drive must come from the pupil.

I hope that this book will prove a rich fountain to all who drink from it.

A final word before getting down to business. When suggesting that any reader will derive better results by using technique A than another reader using technique B please add the words, 'all other things being equal'.

You may have a smoother delivery than your opponent but if his touch and direction are superior he will still win. To become a champion one must pay stringent attention to every vital detail. That demands character, concentration and real eagerness to improve. The mere fact that you have started to read this book shows that you are not devoid of those characteristics. On those foundations you *can* become a champion, perhaps of your club, maybe of your county or country.

Of one thing I can assure you. The efforts you make in striving for your secret goal (your journey) will be at least as exciting and rewarding as its final attainment—the arrival. So give it a real go.

1

Understanding the Green and Your Bowls

Once an essentially recreational game, bowls is now so highly competitive that it is extremely difficult to fit any new tournaments into the annual calendar, whether they are indoor or outdoor events.

The annual English Bowling Championships are divided into four events for which entries now top 70,000 each year and that is but one group of competitions. Tournaments like Weston-super-Mare, Bournemouth, Broadstairs, etc., attract hundreds of players each year.

All entrants have one primary aim—consistently to deliver their bowls nearer to a jack than those of their opponents. Positional play, tactics, end-killing drives, blocks and so on, may sometimes conceal this object but there remains always one unchallengeable fact. The bowl nearest to the jack at the completion of each end is decisive. Bowl one an end and you will win every match you play. The problem is, of course, to deliver that bowl.

To do this you must possess skill and judgement. To some degree these are natural, instinctive talents but no man is so richly endowed that he cannot benefit from greater knowledge and superior practice methods.

Knowledge has many facets and in bowls this should begin with the green and implements. If one travels the world all types of greens are likely to be found. But the majority are grass or, indoors, some form of carpet. Understanding of these should enable the average competitive bowler to adapt to rubber, marl or any of the other unusual surfaces he may meet without undue difficulty.

Most bowlers consider an outdoor green, pleasant opponents and a warm, sunny day their conception of a sporting paradise, but that tranquil, green square is far from being the simple thing many people imagine. How complicated it is may be gathered from Lewis Cave's recommendations for the construction of an E.B.A. type green using Cumberland or sea-washed turf. After writing about clearance and drainage he then specifies a four and a half inch covering of clean clinker and a further covering of four inches of fine clinker, on top of which is superimposed a layer of double-washed sand. Some greens should then have a further layer of compost one and a half inches deep, and finally the turf, which should be laid in diagonal lines, double-washed sand being used to fill any crevices between the turves.

Thus it can be seen that, like an iceberg, the visible part is only about one-eighth of the whole. Since the top itself is capable of many variations, it is easy to realize why greens behave in an infinite variety of ways.

There are many types of grass and they can be sown in many variations of density. The grass itself bends towards the sun, causing the pace of any green to change during the course of a sunny day.

An experienced groundsman mows the green diagonally and this to some extent reduces any likelihood of nap. But there must be a tendency for a bowl to run with the mow once the curve of its course has aligned it with the line taken by the groundsman.

To summarize, these are some of the variables which affect the pace of the green: the condition of the undersurface, the surface itself, the density of the grass, the degree of sunshine, the amount of rain that has fallen in the hours and days before play, the amount of wind, the trueness of laying, the amount of wear—this will be greatest near the ditches where the constant pounding of feet not only wears the grass but also hardens the surface. The length of the grass also has an effect. Public park greenkeepers often wind back the adjusters on their mowers to leave the grass long enough to reduce skilled bowlers to near fury. The classic of this was at Balgreen, Edinburgh, during the 1970 Commonwealth Games where continuous rain and long grass resulted in greens so slow that in countries like Australia and South Africa they would have been judged unfit for play.

The mechanics of the way in which greens and their pace change the performance of bowls is explained later. Meanwhile, indoor greens vary almost as much as those found outdoors. Again, these variations are functions of surface, underlay, heat, air humidity, wear, and how tightly the carpet and underlay is stretched. So far as surfaces are concerned, there are differences between natural and man-made materials. Think for a moment of the relative softness of pure wool and nylon. One is soft and yielding, the other much harder. Transfer that to a bowls green and it will be appreciated that with a natural fabric the bowl will sink in somewhat while with the man-made fibre the bowl will run more on the surface because of its non-yielding nature. True, the underlay must have some effect, but throughout this book when discussing the relative values or performances of 'X' and 'Y' I shall always be implying 'all other things being equal'.

The two primary man-made surfaces used in Britain are Acriturf and Marsward. The former came into being when Colin Brown, a director of a sports field construction company, read a technical report which suggested to him the use of acrilic fibre as the basis for a surface which would retain the best qualities of turf and carpets without any of the disadvantages. One immense benefit which seemed possible was virtual indestructibility. Wear, both of turf and orthodox carpets, is a frighteningly large item in the budget of any club.

Colin Brown liaised with John Jeffrey, head of the Physical Education and Industrial Fitness Unit at Loughborough Uni-

13

versity, in research which eventually resulted in the production of Acriturf.

It was first necessary to specify requirements, the chief of which were playing characteristics and wear. It is understandable that the various weaves and densities they had made and then tested showed great variations in playing characteristics.

What clearly emerged was the immense effect the underlay and tautness of the carpet had on speed, and, therefore, on the degree of curve of a running bowl. The university had available or were able to make sophisticated photo-electric and electronic measuring equipment and this revealed that variations of underlay cause immense differences of pace. Using a chute which gave an exact amount of propulsion each time, the researchers produced variations of 13 to 20 feet runs, a difference of over 50 per cent. In passing, they also arrived at a weave and thickness which permits Acriturf to be used without an underlay providing the basic floor is flat and stable. However, there are some bowlers who claim that man-made fibres are less sensitive to touch than natural carpets of jute or wool or felt.

This is not the place to argue such technicalities. It is sufficient that readers should appreciate there are differences in behaviour and understand why this is so. Such understanding should lead them to increase their adaptability and so their flexibility in changing from surface to surface.

As with outdoor greens, the areas near the ditches are subject to more wear than those in the centre so that few greens play at a uniform pace over their entire area. Broadly speaking, the wear is caused by the pounding of feet. This tends to solidify the under portions of the green as well as the surface itself. The density of the grass is also likely to be reduced. Thus the boundaries of an average green play faster than the centre. In practice, this means that the swing of a bowl delivered from a mat 6 feet from the ditch to a jack say 28 yards away—it will be near the centre of the green—will be appreciably less than from a mat moved 10 yards up the green with the jack still 28 yards away. On a 40-yards-long green the jack will be 2 yards only from

14

the ditch, the green in that area will have had more feet trampling over it and so will be harder and faster. Thus the same bowl delivered with identical power will travel for a longer time, so giving the bias the chance to curve the run more.

The tactical implications of this and the mechanical reasons why bowls of different types and shapes differ in performance will be explained later.

Logically, outdoor greens in areas of heavy rainfall will be softer than those in drier regions of the country and this, theoretically, should influence the type of delivery adopted by any bowler taking up the game.

Most of us have played and/or watched cricket and know that fast bowlers do not achieve the same pin-point accuracy as those with slower deliveries. So it must be in bowls. If the bowl has to be forced away to overcome a heavy green, it is logical that the deliverer must suffer in accuracy when compared to his identical twin playing on a sunbaked, true southern green in the middle of a summer heatwave.

So on heavy greens a naturally powerful man will enjoy a slight advantage compared with someone weaker, while the latter, providing he is of sensitive touch, should score on greens where only the slightest push is necessary to send a bowl to a jack thirty yards or so away.

However, bowls themselves vary considerably and understanding of them should assist you in making the correct choice, or, if you already possess a set, in making the best change.

Fundamentally, there are three types of bowls, wood, hardened rubber, and composition.

The oldest bowls were made of boxwood, holly, oak, and yew but all those woods suffer by comparison with lignum vitae. Introduced into Europe by the Spaniards at the start of the sixteenth century, it did not reach England until about 1694 and there is no record of bowls being made from it until the middle of the eighteenth century.

One of the foremost authorities on the manufacture of such bowls is Bill Millar of Edinburgh and he writes of lignum:

'It comes principally from the West Indies, the very best being grown in San Domingo. There are several varieties, all with a blue flower but the one suitable for bowl making is the variety known as *Guaiacum officinale*.

'The tree is very slow growing and the larger trees are many hundreds of years old. They grow to a height of forty or fifty feet. This variety produces the hardest and densest wood in the world—so heavy that it will sink in water. It weighs approximately three and a half ounces per cubic inch.

'The average log selected for bowl making is something over six feet long and about six to seven inches in diameter and the log will weigh about one and a half hundredweights.

'To produce the best quality bowls it is necessary that the part of the log used should be free from sapwood and be tight in the heart. The height of the log should be at the position of the centre of the bowl as bowls are cut from one log so that they are of uniform weight and colour.

'Lignum vitae contains essential oils and should never be allowed to dry out. Consequently during the cutting and turning the exposed surface of the wood are covered with varnish or heavy grease to keep off the air, otherwise cracks would appear in the end wood. That is why your bowls should always have a protective covering of varnish.

'The grain of lignum is peculiar. There is the ordinary grain running lengthwise of the trunk, but there is another grain radiating from the centre in all directions and it is this grain which gives this timber its outstanding value for bowls making.

'With every part of its body bound together within these radiating fibres there can be neither shrinking nor splitting provided that the timber is well and evenly grown and properly seasoned. This remarkable wood therefore is the base on which we build.'

The selected log is cut to size on a band saw, then shaped to approximate shape on one lathe before receiving more precise attention on another. Delicate touches adjust the bias to make up matched sets of four bowls with identical playing qualities.

16

Not until the formation of the Scottish Bowling Association in 1893 were the sizes and weights of bowls fixed and standardized as they are today. Until 1962 the weight of a bowl was directly related to its size. In November of that year the world governing body of the game, the International Bowling Board, abolished the 'weight for size' rule and, instead, framed a law which stipulates maximum and minimum diameters and maximum and minimum weights but permits them to be mixed in any way a bowler chooses.

This law applies in all full international contests but the British Isles Bowls Council retains the old rule for all its domestic tournaments and championships.

The original rule resulted in some degree from the use of lignum because its virtually fixed density rendered a minimum-size bowl of maximum weight a physical impossibility. Such restrictions do not exist with composition bowls because it is relatively simple to increase or decrease the density of the basic, pre-moulding material.

The bias or imbalance which makes the bowl travel a curved path is created by a slight flattening of one side of the bowl. Until 1893 there was no control of bias but one of the first actions of the Scottish B.A. was to appoint a committee of three noted bowlers, D. Clark, John Scott and James Brown, the first S.B.A. secretary. They asked Thomas Taylor, the Glaswegian bowls maker, to supply a number of new bowls of slightly varying bias.

He turned five different bowls, No. 1 which ran fairly straight, No. 2 with a slightly wider curve, No. 3 with a medium curve (draw) and Nos. 4 and 5 with wide sweeps.

The committee spent a week testing these prototype bowls before adopting No. 3 bias as the standard.

More bowls identical with the standard were produced and officially approved testers each have a 'standard' against which all bowls sent in for testing are measured. The I.B.B. require that every bowl shall be tested every ten years and stamped accordingly. This fact is well known yet it still happens that each year some competitors in the various British championships have their bowls rejected because they have not met the testing requirement. Even in the 1970 Commonwealth Games one player had his bowls rejected by the umpire on this count.

No bowl may be used of lesser bias than No. 3 but there is no restriction on having a bias which turns the bowl more than with No. 3.

Returning to the 'weight for size' rule, in order to meet the requirements it is necessary for lignum bowls to be almost spherical in shape, when viewed from behind when travelling the green.

Composition, having a greater density, enables a given weight to be achieved with less material. The actual 'mix' varies from maker to maker. Henselite, the most widely used, is something like one-third heavier than lignum and so bowls sold under that brand name are markedly elliptical when seen from behind.

Vitalite, the next most popular composition bowl, is made from less dense elements and so its shape approximates more to a lignum than a Henselite. Brewer Industries make a bowl which varies slightly from the others. The significance of shape will be explained later.

The manufacture of composition bowls follows a similar pattern no matter the maker and a complete description of the Henselite system was published in *World Bowls* magazine some years ago. It read: 'Variations in diameter less than one thousandth of an inch; weight variations detectable only on superfine weighing machines used in the minting of money; accuracy of bias and, therefore, track such that the human eye cannot see any difference in finishing position when delivered by a robot bowler. These are the three most spectacular features of Henselite bowls as revealed in a visit to their factory.'

Certainly such bowls have a degree of manufacturing uniformity comparable with that found in a high-grade internal combustion engine. It is on this that the manufacturers of composition bowls all over the world stake their claim to two distinct advantages over lignums, which, they allege, suffer because of (1) the human element in their manufacture and (2) variations in the wood itself plus variations in any one bowl through humidity and temperature changes.

The first of these lignum manufacturers would deny and the second they might well claim as a positive advantage of something which is live—wood—against a dead material, plastic. These arguments will be dealt with in a moment. First, though, a short description of the manufacture of a composition bowl.

The first stage is the weighing out of a precise quantity of the compound which is next machined under extreme pressure into a cylindrical pellet before going to a high-frequency heater.

The pellet is put into a heated mould for shaping into a rough bowl before going on to a special 'slave' lathe which is micrometrically controlled. In this it is shaped to a tolerance finer than one thousandth of an inch.

Another special lathe shaves one side of the bowl in order to give it its bias.

Marking is done on another lathe, a multi-tooled one of special design.

Next comes weighing and testing, collecting into matched sets of four bowls with identical characteristics, smoothing, polishing, colouring and engraving.

Finally comes testing by an automatic deliverer which delivers bowl after bowl along the 30 feet test table with a precision of direction and length utterly beyond the capabilities of any man.

In passing, this form of manufacture is very necessary in Australia where skilled labour is at a premium. When I visited the Slazenger factory in Sydney there were only two skilled workers along the entire production line—and one of those was the painter who added on the pretty identifying emblems. The other gave individual bowls their final touches of finish and accuracy.

Slazengers are now owned by Dunlops who developed a solid rubber bowl when it was first realized that wooden bowls had their deficiencies. Very few are bought nowadays.

Armed with these details about the basic materials and manufacture of bowls, you should now be able fully to understand why they differ in performance and to choose at least the type, lignum or compo, which will best suit your game.

Returning to lignums, these are rounder in shape, the wood is 'live' and possesses an elasticity absent in dead plastic. Because it is round and slightly elastic it will ride more on top of the green than the most popular compos.

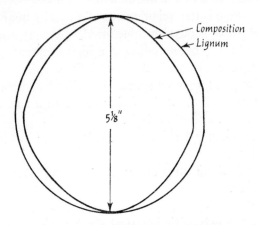

Fig. 1. Lignum has a density of 75 lb. per cubic foot, composition at least 100 lb. per cubic foot. Therefore the compo bowl can be smaller for any given weight. In the case of Henselites the reduction is across the running axis, giving the bowl an elliptical shape when viewed from behind. This makes the running surface sharper, less rounded than a lignum, and the bowl sinks farther into the ground. This gives a braking effect on the sides, tending to resist changes of direction caused by bumps. The braking effect also slows down the run of the bowl more quickly than with lignums, so giving the bias less time to work on (turn) the bowl.

These are elliptical in shape so that the bowl sinks lower into the surface. This added grip on the running surface acts like a brake on a bicycle wheel, causing the bowl to slow down sooner than one of rounder shape and greater natural elasticity. However, it will give the bowl superior stability, both when running and when at rest. Additionally, because the centrifugal centre is nearer to the physical centre than is the case with a wooden bowl, its resistance to change brought about by bumpy surfaces will be greater.

Translating this into dynamic bowls terms, a lignum will travel farther on a heavy green than a compo and so turn more. However, on a hard, low surface-resistance green it will be more difficult to control than a compo, a fact which some experts believe results in the users of lignums eventually developing superior refinements of touch. Harsher critics say that compos help to cover the deficiencies of bad bowlers.

However, because of their reduced surface resistance, lignums are far more easily disturbed by other bowls cannoning into them than compos which sink into the green and can be difficult to dislodge with finessing shots.

On the other hand, on fast surfaces the compos run sufficiently long to give adequate swerve and in Australia and South Africa, where the greens are appreciably faster than in Britain, nearly all bowlers use compos. The generalization, then, is that lignums are better on slow greens and compos on fast greens. But fast and slow are loose descriptive terms. Isn't there some better way of identifying greens of differing characteristics? There is. It is by timing, a system met everywhere in Australia, South Africa and New Zealand to name but three countries. Before detailing how this is done, it would be wise to recall the essential difference between a fast and a slow green.

Like a fast billiards table, a fast bowling green offers minimal resistance to a traversing ball and so it takes longer to come to a stop.

A slow green offers considerable resistance and so the bowl is quickly brought to rest. So in giving a time in seconds a high figure means a fast green and a low figure a slow green.

The distance used in Australia is 30 yards from start to stop. Remember, the bowl is timed from the moment it leaves the deliverer's hand until it finally stops 30 yards up the green, *not* when it passes the 30 yards point; it is surprising how many bowlers make this mistake.

What constitutes a fast green? Those at Kyeemagh, Sydney,

during the inaugural World Championships were treated to give 16 seconds of time from start to stop at 30 yards and were considered fast. Those at Balgreen, Edinburgh, during the 1970 Commonwealth Games, never exceeded $9\frac{1}{2}$ seconds and were cursed for their slowness by the Australians who, back home, would have ruled them 'unplayable'.

Those at Watneys B.C., Mortlake, where the English Bowling Championships are staged each August, vary between 11 and 14 seconds with 12 seconds as a fair average. In New Zealand they can reach 23 seconds, a lightning pace which makes them virtually unplayable; the slightest puff of wind causes the bowl to move, so slight is the surface resistance.

The following table shows the relative times in seconds in which the bowl travelled the first 25 yards and then came to rest at varying lengths on a green timed at 12 seconds for 30 yards during the 1970 E.B.A. Championships at Watneys B.C., Mortlake:

Distance of jack from delivery	25 yards	25 yards to stop	Total
30 yards	$6\frac{1}{4}$	$5\frac{3}{4}$	12
31 ,,	$6\frac{1}{8}$	$6\frac{3}{8}$	$12\frac{1}{2}$
32 ,,	6	7	13
33 ,,	$5\frac{7}{8}$	$7\frac{5}{8}$	$13\frac{1}{2}$
34 ,,	$5\frac{3}{4}$	$8\frac{1}{4}$	14
35 ,,	$5\frac{5}{8}$	$8\frac{7}{8}$	$14\frac{1}{2}$
36 ,,	$5\frac{1}{2}$	$9\frac{1}{2}$	15

These are dynamic measurements made in the finals of championships play.

The times are the average for a great number of deliveries on varied hands; the variations fell well within a range of plus or minus half a second on all distances.

At this pace the average amount of land needed to pull the bowl back to the centre of the rink averaged seven feet. At other sessions when the time for a start to stop over 30 yards rose to 14 seconds the land needed for a return to the middle of the rink varied around a mean of nine feet; in other words, the delivery had to be right out to the string.

The indoor green at Teesside during the 1970 Evening Gazette International Masters tournament ran at 13 seconds for 30 yards when Henselite bowls were used. Again, the timing varied fractionally, depending on the individual characteristics of each set of bowls. The land needed for a swing back to the middle of the rink was: David Bryant, 7 feet 3 inches; Michael London, 7 feet 9 inches; Peter Inch, 7 feet 9 inches; Ken Bainbridge, 8 feet.

Because highly polished lignums possess less surface resistance and greater elasticity they trickle on for a longer period of time, the bias versus forward run effect is increased and the bowl swings far more; in all cases a number 3 bias is under discussion and the bowl is delivered truly.

In theory, on a perfect green the bowl must be delivered at the same angle from the mat, irrespective of the distance of the jack from the mat. In practice, especially when the jack is near to the ditch, the angle has to be changed. This is because the amount of wear on a green affects its pace and, therefore, the length of time the bowl takes over its 'trickle' period. Remember, the longer this time is, the more the bias will bend the final run of the bowl.

This bend can be dramatic, as was seen at Kyeemagh on the 16 seconds greens the Australians prepared for the inaugural World Championships in 1966.

Norman 'Snowy' Walker, the South African maestro, used highly polished Henselite bowls and on occasions these ran on so long that the last inch or so was backwards towards the mat; they had turned almost 180 degrees and finished up touching the back of the jack as viewed from the mat.

These factors set up a number of interesting situations. For example, a successful singles player will have to overcome series of opponents under a great variety of conditions. In England the English Bowling Association Championships are contested by the finalists of the individual championships staged by the thirty-four affiliated counties. These have to be reached by the end of

23

July and with individual entries sometimes topping the 1,000 mark it is necessary to start very early in May or even near the end of April. At that time of the year the turf is usually soft and yielding so that Henselites, to take the extreme in elliptical shape, sink well in and the braking effect on the running surface is considerable. If the green is down to 9 seconds in slowness the amount of swing these bowls will make is significantly limited. Under such conditions a man using lignums will hold a marked advantage in flexibility, all other things being equal. On the other hand, by the end of July, especially if the summer has been dry and hot, the lignums will necessitate considerable finesse of touch and will be dangerously unstable compared with Henselites.

Then there are bowls which lie between these two extremes, Vitalite being possibly the best. These may be the ideal, all the year round compromise. Taking a look at Crown Green bowls, which is extremely popular in the north and which supports a panel of full-time professional players, some of the top experts possess many sets of bowls—I have heard tell of men who own sixteen different sets—and they make the choice when they know the man to be played and the state of the green which is to be used. In the E.B.A. game David Bryant possesses three sets although in the main he restricts himself to using one of two different sets in tournament play. Norman King, winner of gold medals in both the 1958 and 1970 Commonwealth Games, also chooses from one of two sets when playing a match; actually he concentrates on one set for outdoor play and another for the indoor season.

Bowls are not light things to carry around but in these days of widespread car ownership it is not a great hardship to stow three or four sets in the boot.

This suggests that each set will start off with different characteristics. In fact two sets of seemingly identical weight, make, bias, etc. can vary considerably in performance. One set may, on close examination, have a greater surface polish which reduces resistance and so allows the bowls to trickle on longer than those of the other set. And more trickle means more curve in the full-length run.

Extra curve can be a disadvantage or an advantage, depending on the circumstances. For example, the lead in a fours match normally has one task only, to deliver his bowls nearer to the jack than those of his opposite number. The shortest path to any object is a straight line. Thus many leads track down and buy the straightest running set they can find. Inevitably, they will be number three bias (the lowest permissible) but number three bias bowls can follow varying degrees of straightness, as anyone who cares to try a lignum, Vitalite, and Henselite of same diameter, weight and bias markings can quickly discover on the green.

The final choice lies with each individual and, certainly, no recommendation can be made here, except to recommend that any seriously ambitious bowler fits himself out with at least two sets of bowls—three sets would be better. Two of the sets should, perhaps, carry the same measurements but the third could, with advantage, differ—a larger diameter for use on ultra fast greens, perhaps. Remember, it is championship wins that are being analysed here.

Relating this to the actual bowls used in the inaugural World Championships at Kyeemagh, altogether exactly 100 sets were used. They broke down into the following sizes: $4\frac{7}{8}$ in. diameter, 4; $4\frac{15}{16}$ in., 18; 5 in., 51; $5\frac{1}{16}$ in., 16; $5\frac{1}{8}$ in., 11. Ideally one should have also measured the hand shape and size of every competitor but this simply wasn't possible; logging the bowls sizes was in itself a major operation. Nevertheless, the preponderance of 5-inch bowls is significant.

Those used by the gold medal winners were: David Bryant $5\frac{1}{16}$ in., Bert Palm $4\frac{15}{16}$ in., Geoff Kelly $5\frac{1}{16}$ in., Athol Johnson 5 in., Don Collins 5 in., John Dobbie $5\frac{1}{16}$ in., Ron Buchan 5 in., Gordon Jolly 5 in., Norman Lash 5 in., William O'Neill $4\frac{15}{16}$ in.

There are two schools of thought concerning the size of bowl a man should use. One of them specifically relates the hand-finger stretch to diameter. This is achieved by letting the tips of one's two thumbs and middle fingers make a circle around the running circumference of a bowl, the ideal size being when those tips just meet.

It is a popular system but it ignores the possibility that a man's two hands may differ slightly in size. Thus, if the span of the right thumb and second finger is greater than that of the left thumb and second finger, the bowl is theoretically too small while if the left hand is smaller, the bowl is too large.

Returning to the performance of any bowl on a green, it has been shown why there is a longer 'trickle' period on a fast green than on a slow one. Translating this to practicalities, this means that on a slow, 10 seconds green a good drawing shot will leave the bowl 3 inches from the jack; on a fast, 16 seconds green the extended 'trickle to a stop' part of the bowls roll means that tiny variations in touch have an appreciable effect on the distance from the jack at which the bowl finishes. Thus anything within 12 inches of the jack can be deemed a good draw.

Consequently, a fast green is considerably more responsive to refinements of touch than one so resistant that the finishing trickle of a bowl's run is severely restricted.

In the former playing conditions it is necessary for the bowl to leave the fingers and hand in precisely the same way in delivery after delivery, and, perhaps, this is inhibited slightly by thumb pressure, a little extra adding a slight braking effect, a little less pressure reducing braking.

So some say it helps to lessen thumb effect by using slightly oversize bowls, measured by the thumbs and second fingers measuring system.

Just as the thumb is basically a 'steadier' rather than a 'pusher' of the bowl, so is the little finger, but if it creeps too far up the side of the bowl the palm of the hand suffers slight distortion. This, almost inevitably, leads to wobble.

The second finger exercises most influence on the direction of delivery and this finger should be central, or almost central, on the running surface with the third finger in close support. Each individual must experiment until he discovers the grip that suits

26

him best—but what is best? Possibly the grip which gives most control over direction, since a bowl directly in front of or behind the jack is likelier to become effective than one lying way out at the side of the head.

Finally, the jack. This is the white, $2\frac{1}{2}$ inches (approximately) white ball weighing between 8 and 10 ounces which forms the centre of the overall target. On fast greens indoors the standard weight given above does not provide sufficient stability; a relatively light touch sends it careering off the rink. So the English Indoor Bowling Association and its sister bodies have approved a jack weighing twice that of outdoor jacks for use in all competitions staged under their auspices. It is not biased although jacks used in the Crown Green game so popular in Lancashire and Yorkshire are made with an imbalance—bias.

Now to relate all these facts to actual play.

2

Grip and Delivery

Returning for a moment to the object of bowls, it is to roll one's bowls up the green so that they finish nearer to the jack than the opponent's. Each bowl nearer to the jack, than the nearest (best) of the opponent's scores a point.

Actual delivery is made from, or with one foot over, a mat 24 inches long and 14 inches wide. After the first end the back edge of the mat shall be not less than 4 feet from the rear ditch, and the front edge not less than 27 yards from the front ditch, and on the centre line of the rink of play. The jack must not be less than 6 feet from the front ditch when an end begins nor less than 25 yards from the front of the mat.

On a green 42 yards long, therefore, the longest starting position of the jack from the front of the mat must be 38 yards— (back edge of mat from ditch 4 feet plus length of mat 2 feet plus jack from far ditch 6 feet equals 12 feet (4 yards); 4 yards from 42 yards equals 38 yards).

The shortest jack, as stipulated by the rules, is 25 yards. The difference between 38 and 25 is 13 and 13 (the difference) over 25 (the shortest jack) equals 52 per cent, a considerable variation when considered in terms of the power that must be used in delivering the bowl. This is of great tactical importance when a bowler of sensitive touch is playing one lacking in this vital quality; but more of that later.

Having gathered some conception of the variations which exist in bowls and green surfaces, it should not be difficult to realize that your personal mechanics should be as regular as possible. In other words, the smoother and more regular you make your technique of delivering the bowl, the better your chance of neutralizing the other variables—and of winning, all other things between you and your opponent being equal. If, like David Bryant, you support splendid technique with sensitive touch and unwavering applied concentration you will win far more matches than you lose.

First, then, it is necessary to understand the two fundamental ways in which the bowl can be held prior to delivery: the grips. These are the claw and the cradle. You will hear many others in discussion but they are only variations of the claw or the cradle.

In the claw grip the bowl rests on your hand, your fingers fitting round it like a claw. They are slightly spread, with the little finger below the little disc and the thumb just above the opposite disc; on heavy greens, where it is necessary to grip the bowl tighter in order to obtain sufficient thrust, the thumb may be right on top of the bowl. In general, the slower the green, the higher it is necessary to put the thumb.

As with the cradle grip, it is vital for the bowl to rest on the palm of the hand. If there is any kind of gap between palm and bowl there is a danger of pulling the fingers across the bowl during delivery and, thus, of imparting wobble to it.

With the claw grip the feel is of pushing the bowl away. In the cradle grip the bowl sits in the cup of the palm, the thumb and little finger contacting the bowl around the lower circumference of the grip ring.

This results in the index, middle and fourth fingers being closer together than with the claw and the feel is of rolling the bowl out of the hand with a minimum of friction. This enables the finger-tips—the most sensitive part of the human body—to impart the gentlest nuances of touch. Thus the cradle grip is ideally suited to fast greens—those of 14 seconds or faster. If the green is ultra fast, say over 16 seconds, the wrist can be held in a more definite cupped position, the bowl rested further forward on the track lines between the fingers so that the bowl slides gently out of the hand. In all cases the middle two fingers exercise the greatest effect on direction and the thumb on length.

Normally the bowl is held so that the discs on the two sides of the bowl are parallel when the bowl begins its run up the green.

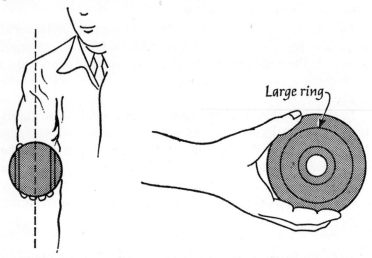

Fig. 2. The position of the fingers when gripping a bowl. The higher up the thumb, the firmer the grip but the more consistency is effected by tension.

There are some bowlers who hold the bowl so the bias is not perpendicular to the green. By tilting the bowl they make the bias rotate and so reduce its effect. This can be reasonably effective with lignums because they are virtually spherical in shape. But compositions, especially Henselites, are markedly elliptical when viewed from behind so that if they are delivered with a tilt they will run bumpity-bump instead of smoothly over the green. This results in an inaccuracy which negatives the benefit of tilt.

Percy Baker is one of the great bowlers who make significant use of tilt but he uses lignums. Very few top-class bowlers recommend tilting; they prefer to correct the run of their bowls by adjustments of delivery positions on the mat.

There are four recognized methods of actually delivering a bowl: (1) the kneeling position, (2) the crouch, (3) the semi-crouch and, (4) the upright—sometimes called the athletic.

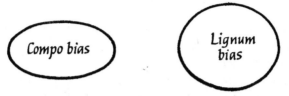

Fig. 3. The exaggerated diagram shows how tilting reduces or eliminates the curve of a bowl's run caused by bias, but how the elliptical shape of some compos causes a bumpy run, and therefore inaccuracy. Lignum bowls are more suited to tilting. The drawings exaggerate the shapes.

Old illustrations, notably the one in Strutt's *Sports and Pastimes of the People of England,* depict bowlers with their right knees right on the ground. Nowadays this delivery is seldom seen, although Danny Winning of the Blackhall, Durham, E.B.A. Fours Championship 1970 winning team uses it. For good reason: a police officer, he was returning home one evening when he saw a thug attacking an old lady. In rescuing her he sustained an injury which forced him to give up cricket, wear a steel back support and to take to bowls. This is the only delivery he can manage but, as the E.B.A. records show, this has not stopped him from collecting one major honour.

This particular form of delivery is suited to very fast greens but the lack of body thrust means that all power is developed through the arm and this is insufficient, except with excessive strain, for overcoming slow surfaces. One still sees elderly men delivering in this manner, but, nowadays, it has largely given way to the semi- and full-crouch systems. Descriptions of these will follow but, first, the upright should be outlined because that is the delivery taught in the successful 'Bowls for Beginners' courses staged by many County Associations nowadays. These courses really are splendid for absolute beginners and I strongly recommend any non-playing readers who are about to take up the game to enrol for one at the first possible moment. Rather than give a long list of names and addresses of county secretaries I will list only the Central Council of Physical Recreation, 26 Park Crescent, London, W1N 4AJ. They will supply details.

Still with beginners in mind, I am reproducing a section of the useful booklet produced by the Hertfordshire Bowling Association, a copy of which is given to each man enrolling in their scheme. The relevant section concerns delivery and first covers grips. It then moves on to stance and reads: 'The feet should be together, pointing along the line on which the bowl is to travel,

Fig. 4. Typical stance when beginning the upright (athletic) delivery.

knees relaxed and elbows slightly bent, body leaning slightly forward at approximately 30 degrees from vertical, bowl held out in front of the body on a line just outside the right hip to allow a clean swing down outside the right leg; eyes looking along the delivery line to a convenient point on the green, weight forward on the balls of the feet, not back on the heels, with most of the weight carried on the right foot.

'Now, having got the correct relaxed posture, transfer to the mat for a forehand draw.'

Footwork. 'The importance of footwork cannot be too

32

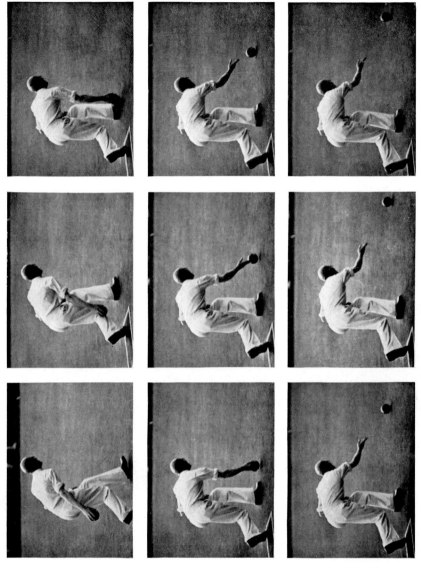

Plate 1.
Complete
delivery by
Norman King.

Plate 2. The start of David Bryant's delivery.

Plate 3. Note how turning the hand inwards by an angle of 45 degrees enables world champion David Bryant's arm to swing in a completely straight line. This, he asserts, assists his accuracy.

strongly stressed. Like all other ball games, the feet play a vital part in direction and consistency.

'Irrespective of type of delivery, taking a step or adopting a fixed stance, the feet and body must be facing the grass line.

'If a step is taken, it must be along the grass line, if a fixed stance, then the feet must be placed along the grass line.

'When delivering a bowl, the hand will naturally follow the front foot; if the foot is placed in the wrong direction, the hand will want to follow that foot, thus an ill-directed bowl will result.

'With the bowl in the right hand, step on to the mat and place the right foot about six inches from the front edge of the mat, and about three inches from the right-hand side, and line it in with the grass line pointing to the aiming point. With the right foot in this position, pointing along the line on which the bowl is to be delivered, bring the left foot alongside the right, feet together but not strained; now the feet and body should be facing towards the aiming point.

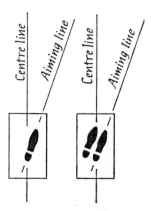

Fig. 5. Positioning of feet for forehand draw.

'Having achieved this position see that the right hip is slightly behind the left. This clears the right hip out of the way and allows for a clean swing down past the right leg; it also places the body in position for the step forward with the left foot. If the right hip is held too far forward, the left foot, when taking

C   33

the forward step, will be forced wide of the grass line and a narrow bowl will result.'

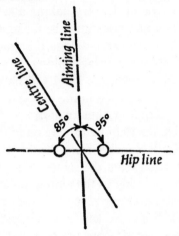

Fig. 6. Axis of hips when beginning delivery.

Back swing. 'Now you are ready for the down or back swing; the pace of this is regulated by the position in which the bowl is held in front of you, i.e. low for a short end just below hip-high for a medium end and hip-high for a long end, of course taking into account the pace of the green.'

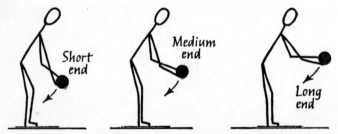

Fig. 7. Variation in length of back swing for short, medium and long ends. The strength of delivery should be governed by the length of the back swing, not by any variation in speed of down swing.

Down swing. 'If possible, allow the bowl to drop under its own weight; this will ensure a smooth back swing—do not drag the bowl back.

'In detail: start the back swing by allowing the bowl to drop under its own weight, the swing should only travel as far as its own weight will carry it, do not force the bowl back, the arm must be as relaxed as possible, and the back swing kept to a minimum.

'At the same time as the bowl starts to drop, start the left foot moving forward along the line of delivery or grass line, take a natural walking step, no longer.

'As the left foot finds its position along the grass line the back swing should be completed and the weight of the body transferring to the front foot.'

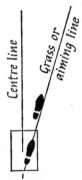

Fig. 8. The line of the delivery and of the two feet should be the same as the line of the delivery.

Left hand. 'As the step forward commences the left hand should be used to achieve perfect balance or transferred to the left knee cap. In either case the arm should be relaxed and used only as a steadying factor.'

Forward swing. 'As the forward swing is carried out the right knee is bent low behind the left heel, weight of the body over the front foot. The bowl is delivered or grassed about nine inches ahead of the left foot, the fingers should almost touch the grass at the point of delivery. The right hand follows through along the line after the bowl. At the completion of the follow through the palm of the hand should be facing upwards about two feet above the green with the fingers pointing along the grass line.

35

Fig. 9. The various stages of delivery. Note that right lower leg is almost parallel with the ground.

'To complete the movement, when the bowl has travelled some six feet up the green, bring the right foot up to the left; this should bring you to a standing position and ready to move off the mat.'

Follow through. 'A smooth follow through is a must and at the finish of the swing the palm of the hand should face upwards, the fingers pointing along the line of delivery. This ensures that the bowl will rotate on an even keel without wobble and will travel along the selected line. As the bowl is grassed the head should be steady and over the foot and grass line. Do not lift the head until the bowl has travelled some six feet along the green.

'*Note.* Footwork is also a must. Unless you take up the correct stance and position on the mat, with the feet pointing along the selected line on which the bowl is to travel for draw, running shot or drive, inconsistency will result. Indeed, as the pace of the shot increases, the value of footwork becomes more important; the player who neglects this will play under a handicap. Therefore look to your footwork before thinking of delivering the bowl.'

For the backhand draw. 'Take up your position on the mat in the same manner as for the forehand draw but, in this case, line the left foot up with the grass line or aiming point and place the right foot against the left. With the start of the swing, place the left foot along the grass line.'

Individual faults. 'Having established the basis for a good delivery, now examine some of the faults that can creep into your game unless closely watched.

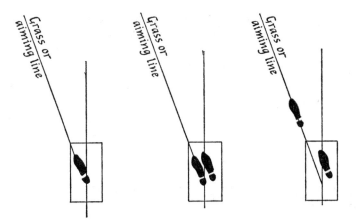

Fig. 10. The line up of the feet for and during a backhand draw shot.

'The following list sets out a few of the most common faults that can develop unless checked at once:
(1) Lack of good footwork (see instruction on footwork).
(2) Placing the front foot off-line.
(3) Delivering the bowl with body parallel to the green with rear leg more or less straight.
(4) The wobbling bowl.
(5) Bending the elbow at end of swing.
(6) The flicker.
(7) Lack of follow through.
(8) The croucher.
(9) Weight on back foot.
(10) Playing too fast.'

Those, then, are the vital passages relating to delivery in the Herts book and they are used by the county coaches when teaching newcomers. There is no need to elaborate on them here because they should have implanted a reasonable conception of the upright delivery. Before refining this delivery the others must be considered, beginning with the crouch.

In this the bowler squats nearly to his haunches, his left leg forward, his right leg doubled beneath him. This somewhat cramped position is, nevertheless, functionally stable and so makes for a reasonable degree of regularity when delivering.

Against this, there is no forward body thrust and the arm swing is less rhythmic than with the upright delivery. This is no great handicap on fast greens when only a slight swing is necessary to propel a bowl 30 or 35 yards. But when rain has made the green heavy full length can only be obtained through forcing the swing and this destroys accuracy and consistency. Today the full crouch is not seen very often although it is probably better suited to elderly players who have lost some of their youthful flexibility of body and leg, and to men suffering from physical disabilities.

There is a good compromise between the upright and full crouch, namely the semi-crouch. In this compromise delivery the bowler takes up position with his right foot on the mat, heel raised and with the left foot a convenient stretch in front of the mat; it is bent roughly at right angles and, as used so splendidly by Tom Fleming, a 1962 Commonwealth Games gold medallist, the arm swings in pendulum fashion. Upon delivery, a bowler using this method rises to an upright position.

Though there is greater thrust compared with the full crouch, the arm and body both suffer some restriction of follow through. Although this style can be recommended to bowlers who, for one reason or another, feel unable to use the upright delivery, it still suffers some disadvantages compared with the upright when used on heavy greens, unless the bowler is tall and with the length of arm of Fleming.

No matter what type of delivery is used, head position is vital. Walk round in a circle and you will soon realize that it is the head and shoulders which determine direction. Turn the head

38

and the whole body tends to turn in sympathy. Lift the head and the whole body tends to tilt backwards. So it is when delivering a bowl, yet it is commonplace to see bowlers jerking up head and, consequently, shoulders while delivery is being made. So keep that head down, if necessary counting five after the bowl has left your hand, before you let your arm relax from the follow through and your head and eyes look up.

The follow through is important no matter whether you swing the bowl down the green as if your arm is a pendulum or if you use a curtailed back swing and develop your power with an arm thrust made by straightening the arm from a bent elbow position to one that is straight during the short period when the bowl is being released from your hand.

The pendulum-type swing lends itself to a cradle grip rather more readily than the push-type delivery. In turn, the cradle grip enables the bowl to be rolled from the hand naturally or even with a slight forward spin (the top of the bowl is rotating slowly in the same direction as its travel) while with the push delivery and claw grip there is a tendency to give thrust to the under-part of the bowl, thus causing some skid during the first part of its run.

This can be advantageous on very fast greens but where a bowl will tend to leave the hand uniformly when rolled, the skid of a push-claw delivered bowl will vary slightly depending on the strength of the claw grip; and one of the difficult variables of bowls is the degree nervous tension affects the strength of the grip.

Such variations may be slight and more than counter-balanced by superior skills in other directions. But, as in all comparisons made in this book, the implied phrase is 'all other things being equal'.

Another point it is necessary to make is that once a bowler has reached, say, county team standard he is unlikely suddenly to discover some new and vital factor and so improve dramatically overnight. They say 'tall oaks from little acorns grow', which I amend in this case to 'great bowls improvement from attention to many little details comes'. If one month of thoughtful and purposeful practice can improve you 5 per cent a month—that is one shot in a 21-up singles—you will be 50 per cent improved by the end of two summers—that is the equivalent of 10 shots in that same singles. By any reckoning that is a massive advance.

Returning to the different types of delivery, the upright is the smoothest and most easily adaptable to any type of green but with one important rider. The deliverer must be supple, especially at the hips and in the knees, and possess good balance. This is governed to some extent by the strength and flexibility of his legs. If you are stiff kneed and suffer from any back aches or pains and your natural sense of balance is uncertain, you will probably develop greater accuracy through delivering your bowls from the more stable base of a semi-crouch delivery.

Not that movement of the body inevitably means instability. Smooth movement is as stable as an unchanged position but with the body movement inherent in an upright delivery a creaking back and knees so easily transfer jerks to the swing.

So if you are sure your leg strength and flexibility plus your suppleness in other parts of your body plus your sense of balance and rhythm when swinging your delivery arm are satisfactory, use the upright delivery, perhaps as detailed earlier in this chapter, maybe in the modified manner evolved by that master thinker of bowls, World Champion David Bryant.

He begins his basic, draw shot on a normal paced green from a crouch position but as his arm swings back he straightens his legs slightly, slipping his left forward rather than stepping as in the orthodox upright delivery.

The amount he rises, the distance he slides his left foot forward, and the length of his back swing are all governed by the pace of the green and the distance of the jack from the front of the mat. If the green is fast and the jack only a bare 25 yards away his rise will be extremely slight, his back swing almost non-existent and the slide forward of his left foot not much more than 12 inches. On the other hand, on a slow green he will rise almost to the upright position, his back swing will be long and his left foot forward movement as long as a full step. Indeed, on ultra-slow greens or when firing at the head he abandons his preliminary crouch and starts from the upright position.

This use of the legs and, particularly, the sliding forward of the foot without any wavering or loss of balance demands very strong leg muscles as well as flexibility and Bryant is aware that he will have to abandon this system of delivery when the passing years diminish his strength or flexibility. But while he retains the qualities of a young man this method gives him impressive sensitivity of touch when imparting minute changes of strength to his deliveries. It also enables him to alternate full-blooded firing shots with gentle draw shots without the former blunting his touch for the latter.

Another subtle point about delivery is the arm itself. Most advocates of the upright delivery specify that the palm of the hand should be facing up the green at the moment the bowl is released and should still be looking along the delivery line at the end of its follow through.

Put this book down for a moment, stand up and let your arm hang by your side with the palm facing straight ahead. Does your arm feel comfortable? Is there not a strain centred about the elbow?

Now let your hand turn inwards somewhat, say by 45 degrees. Your arm should now be freed from any feeling of strain. Now look at yourself in a full-length mirror. With the palm looking ahead your arm will not look straight but by turning the palm inwards you will reach a stage where the arm appears straight. This straightness will remain while your arm swings, pendulum fashion, backwards and forwards as in delivering a bowl. Again, all other things being equal, a straight swing should give you an advantage over a bowler delivering with a forearm which is not at precisely 90 degrees with the green's surface.

Such an inward turning of the arm entails a problem in getting a bowl away so that the bias is exactly to the side. With the 'palm forward' swing the middle finger of the delivery hand is positioned along the centre of the bowls running surface. With the hand turned in grip the fourth (ring) finger takes over this position or, rather, the lower knuckle of it does. It is also necessary to ensure that the turn remains constant throughout the swing.

There is a danger when the arm begins its swing from a turned-in position for it to turn further during the latter part of that swing. Clearly, the swing cannot affect the path of a bowl that has left the hand but in all probability the twist will have started before the bowl has been grassed. So it will have a slight twist from right to left and that will tend to swing the bowl from right to left over the last one or two yards of its run.

Note that the arm twist will almost certainly be from right to left—rather like a right hook delivered by a 'southpaw' boxer. This must be countered—and long before any important match is played. The place to correct faults is on the practice green. Once any match has begun all concentration should be applied to the positional plays and tactics necessary to beat the opponent; your actual deliveries should be subconscious.

Quoting the 'Bowls for Beginners' instructions earlier in this chapter, they advocate pulling the right hip back slightly before delivery to allow a clean swing of the arm. In golf and tennis that instruction is supplemented by a further one to push the hip round and through ahead of the actual swing, again to get it out of the way of the arm. Now, many successful bowlers place the left hand on the left knee during the swing. Try this and you will discover that it assists stability but severely restricts body turn.

If the golf and tennis precept is to be followed—and there is a scientific reason for suggesting it should be—the left arm must be swung out of the way. So stand up and try an imaginary delivery. Let your arm swing back as though you were handling a bowl. Then, just as you start the forward swing, thrust the right hip forward ahead of the down-swinging right arm and let the left arm swing backwards past the left side. Probably if you attempt this on the green itself you will find some difficulty in obtaining regularity of control, especially of length. Yet I will wager that you will find it easier to swing the arm in an absolutely straight line. Probably you will settle down to the left hand on knee system but this knowledge of how the hip helps straightness should persuade you consciously to try for a little body turn, particularly when lining up your delivery.

Many—most even—bowlers try to maintain contact between mat and back foot long after the bowl has left the hand. This also reduces body thrust and imposes some slight and unnatural strain. Watch David Bryant when he is, say, 18–14 down and facing a two-shot deficit when he delivers his last bowl. His right leg will float upwards during the follow through until it is parallel with the ground, his left and right hand taking up the balance by touching the ground in front of him as though in the start of a 100 yards sprint.

It is all part of a rhythmic, floating delivery that avoids all jerks and strains and that is what you must always seek. George Warman, a left hander, produced a wonderful example of back leg up with the delivery—the last of the match—which snatched victory from defeat to win the Denny Cup for Cyphers back in 1965.

Two other tips may help you to counter the tendency to lift the head, and thus the shoulders and body, during delivery. The first is to count five after the bowl has left your hand—right on the green, please; no bumping, ever—before looking at the jack. The other is to follow your delivery a few steps up the green. If it really is flowing you will be unlikely to deliver, straighten up, and then start running.

Bowlers vary somewhat in what they look at when the bowl leaves the hand. On the whole, they tend first to look from bowl to the shoulder of the line they hope to achieve, then back to the bowl, then to the shoulder and to keep their eyes on that point during the forward swing and moment of loosening the bowl. Championship winning bowlers will exercise such control over their nerves that they will continue to look along that line for some seconds after delivery. Over-anxious players look up immediately, often while the bowl is still in hand. So before the actual delivery first imagine it in detail—and as a success. This mental rehearsal is practised by top golfers and tennis players and is a recognized psychological factor in successful execution of motor skills like delivering a bowl.

Direction and length are equally important in theory but in

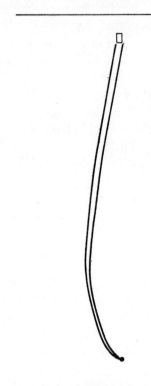

Fig. 11. The diagram, drawn to exact scale and using a template to ensure the paths of two similar bowls delivered with the same power follow identical curvatures, shows that by using the width of the mat there is considerable scope for avoiding obstacles. By varying the length of mat used, the flexibility of path becomes extremely high. To deliver on the forehand round a bowl in the course one wishes to take, bowl from the left-hand side of the mat; to deliver inside it, use the right-hand side of the mat. Going round the outside of a stopper, use fractionally less power. Aiming inside it, reduce power a shade.

actual play even a Bryant delivers many moderate bowls. If they are off course they are much more unlikely to shift into the count than if they are in line with the jack though short or long in length. So strive always for direction, bearing in mind that your bowl will turn more over its last yard of run if the jack is near the ditch than when it is some yards up the green.

Correction of length may be obtained by slight changes in the swing, by slight use of the middle finger; it is surprising how much effect a subtle, minute flick can achieve. But remember that the mat is 24 inches long and 14 inches wide and there is nothing to stop you bowling from any part of it.

By bowling from different spots on the mat you can change the path of your bowls so that they avoid obstacles or vary in length by a couple of feet—and all with the identical strength and direction, relative to your body, of delivery.

Eventually each bowler must arrive at his own style of delivery by experimenting until he discovers one best suited to his build and temperament.

However, it is possible to gather some idea of the most suitable style by studying experts and I had this in mind at the 1965 Hilton Cup International Match series. Then I carefully analysed the entire England team, the results coming out as follows:

Gordon Sparks: Very tall and thin build. Upright delivery with long step forward at end of back swing which is almost continuous with forward swing. Long follow through with body well down. Thumb three-quarters up.

Harold Burbage: Tall, medium build. Crouch delivery with legs well spread. Thumb half-way up bowl which rolls out of hand.

Ken Freeman: Medium height and build. Left hander. Starts delivery upright but front foot grounded before back swing begins. Cradle grip, thumb well down.

Peter Brimble: Medium height, medium to slim build. Upright delivery with short, abrupt swing containing a fair amount of 'shovel'. Bowl away off floor. Back and forward swing continuous, front foot grounded at start of forward swing. Cradle grip, thumb well down.

George Shoobridge: Young, small, slim built. Upright delivery, then down slowly with slow back swing and slow, controlled forward step. Finger grip, thumb seven-eighths of way towards top.

Sid Bond: Tallish, plumpish build. Upright delivery with slight pause between back and forward swing. Shortish follow through. Thumb on top.

Arthur Owen: Tallish, medium build. Starts upright . . . then goes down . . . then delivers. Shortish back swing and pause. Longish, straight follow through.

Harry Kneebone: Medium height and build. Upright delivery. Slight pause between back and forward swing. Thumb on top. Slight pushing action.

Gilbert Attwood: Medium height and build. Upright delivery with front foot grounded before start of forward swing. Pronounced pause between back and forward swing. Thumb about three-quarters towards top.

Harry Pook: Upright delivery with front foot grounded at start of back swing. Medium height and build. Bowl fairly well into hand and thumb high up.

Chick Tanner: Medium height, plumpish build. Upright delivery, cradle grip with thumb slightly below centre of bowl.

Vic Oliver: Small, slight build. Upright, brisk delivery with front foot grounding as forward swing begins. Scarcely perceptible pause between back and forward swings. Finger grip, thumb mid-way between the two rings (above centre).

Len Kirton: Tallish man, slim build. Starts in the upright position but after sighting goes down for full-crouch. Thumb grip is three-quarters towards top of bowl.

Harry Haynes: Medium height and build. Touches ground with bowl, then rises to full height. Delivers from upright stance start, his front foot going down as back swing begins. Uses finger grip with thumb at side.

Jim Girdwood: Tall, slim build. Begins delivery in upright

46

position but front foot is down before swing begins. Uses cradle grip, thumb half-way up.

David Bryant: Medium height and build. Unique delivery best described as athletic but with the height of the body rise and the length of the stride varied to suit the length of the shot. Finger grip, thumb well on top.

Bill Taylor: Medium height and build. Stands upright before he bends for delivery with the forward step co-ordinated with the back swing. Uses cradle grip, thumb half-way up.

Sid Martin: Short to medium height, medium build. Left hander. Full-crouch delivery. Cradle grip, thumb well down.

Jim Brayley: Medium height, medium to plumpish build. Upright delivery with swing back co-ordinated with front foot going forward. Distinct pause between back and forward swing. Uses finger grip with thumb three-quarters of way to top of bowl.

Norman King: Tall, slim build. Upright delivery with front foot grounding as back swing begins. Uses cradle grip with thumb well down bowl.

Alan Bates: Medium to tall, heavy build. Crouch delivery made with shovel arm action. Goes down to sight, then bobs up and down slightly while delivering. Thumb three-quarters of way to top of bowl.

Bill Edgar: Tallish, slimmish build. Upright stance, the front foot grounding at the start of the forward swing which is continuous with back swing. Thumb well on top.

Arthur Knowling: Short to medium, plumpish build. Upright delivery, front foot grounding as forward swing begins. Thumb on top.

John Scadgell: Tall, slim build. Upright delivery. Back and forward swing continues, the front foot grounding as forward swing commences. Thumb well on top.

3

Fit for Bowls

Though bowls is becoming ever more a game in which young men participate—and very successfully: for example John Thomas, indoor champion of Wales aged 22; Mike London, conqueror of David Bryant when also 22 years old—it remains essentially a game which men take to when approaching their forties and go on playing into the eighties and even the nineties.

To advocate the kind of training undertaken by, say, a professional soccer player or championship tennis player would be quite stupid. Yet I do believe it is necessary for ambitious bowlers to consider themselves as athletes rather than social relaxers. To that extent I believe they should pay some attention to training, albeit in rather a passive kind of way unless they really are very ambitious and proud of their own performances. Diet, sleep, feet are three important factors in fitness for bowls and I am using acknowledged experts to deal with some of these specialized topics, beginning with diet.

Dr. R. U. Quereshi, M.Sc., Ph.D. (London), F.I.F.S.T., is an acknowledged expert on diet and I am indebted to him for the following treatise on the nutritional needs of a bowls player.

'The degree of physical fitness of a player depends upon his health and the state of his nutrition. A good diet balanced with respect to its nutrients affords better health. It would be a hard task, and probably unfair, to compose a diet for a bowls player and generalize it as a panacea for best results. A good diet is mainly composed of proteins, fats, carbohydrates, minerals and vitamins. These five constituents are present in most of our customary dishes and a complete meal is derived from the choice of these dishes. An average British diet provides about 76·5 g. (2·6 oz.) of protein, 118 g. (4·2 oz.) of fat and 343 g. (12 oz.) of carbohydrate per day. It is a matter of common knowledge that the food we eat is metabolized in our bodies to keep us warm, maintain our body weight, support growth and meet with the daily demands of wear and tear on our tissues. All these functions can be expressed in terms of energy utilization which can be calculated from the amount and type of food eaten and measured as calories of heat. In these terms our average British diet gives a total of 2,650 calories per person per day, of which carbohydrates contribute about 48 per cent, fat about 40 per cent and proteins about 11 per cent.

'In such a diet the chief source of calories would be carbohydrate in all its forms, such as sweets, cakes, biscuits, puddings, potatoes and bread. Proteins come largely from all kinds of meat, fish, eggs, bread, milk and cheese. The main sources of fat are margarine, butter, cooking oils, dairy products and meat.

'From the nutritional point of view carbohydrates are regarded as energy yielding foods, each gram of which equals roughly 4 calories. Fats are a concentrated form of energy, giving about 9 calories per gram. Proteins are important as body-building constituents in our food, but if used for energy each gram of protein provides about 4 calories. In a mixed diet, such as the British diet, minerals like calcium and iron, and vitamins, for example A, D, B1, B2 and C, are present in ample amounts to meet with the ordinary requirements of most individuals. An average British diet is adequate for an average British person but in practice averages seldom exist. People do not look alike, grow alike or eat alike. Dietary requirements of one group of the population differ from those of other groups of the population; for example, men require more food than women. The dietary requirements within a group also vary considerably, for instance, two bowls players playing the same number of ends a day may have widely differing dietary requirements. There are certain well defined criteria from which it is possible to obtain a good idea of one's caloric and protein requirements. People normally eat enough to satisfy their appetites, which are sated if enough calories are consumed. It is of course possible to satisfy appetite without consuming the required protein, vitamin and mineral needs, but if, as is usually the situation in countries such as our own, a varied diet is consumed the mixture of foods so provided will amply supply the body's needs for all the varied nutrients. A diet of steaks and beer alone would be as bad as one of potatoes and cream cakes; fortunately most people find such diets monotonous, and given the chance, will eat a variety of foods so that in the mixture eaten during the course of the day all the nutrients needed may be met even though none of the foods consumed would, by themselves, supply all the components essential for life and health.

'In Britain and the other affluent countries, proteins in the diet come from various sources. In our average national consumption of proteins, about 60 per cent are derived from animal sources, such as milk, eggs, fish and meat, and the rest come from vegetable sources, largely wheat and potatoes. As a rule, the utilization and thus quality of animal proteins from mixed sources is higher than proteins from vegetable sources. Where the concentration of proteins in a diet is much higher than the requirements, the excess proteins are utilized as energy just like from carbohydrates. The proteins are more expensive than the carbohydrates, therefore excessive amount of protein in a diet is not good value for money. On the other hand, if the concentration of proteins in a diet is low, functions such as growth, body building and repair of the tissues is impaired. An average adult male requires 1·4 grams and an average adult female requires 1·3 grams of mixed proteins per kilogram of body weight. Protein requirements expressed as grams per day for an average sized man and woman would be about 90 grams (3·2 oz.) and 72 grams (2·5 oz.) respectively. Taking protein and calories requirements into account, the concentration of mixed proteins in a diet should range from 10 to 12·5 per cent. The average British diet contains 11·0 per cent proteins and is, therefore, quite adequate from the point of view of protein requirements.'

Dr. Quereshi points out that energy requirements vary considerably from activity to activity. In bowls they vary from man to man, between, for example, a perpetual 'chaser up the green' and a deliverer who stays by the mat.

Additionally, a man's everyday work may be more 'physical' than his game of bowls so that it is impossible to generalize. Nevertheless, as a reasonable average, the excess energy expenditure during a championship or tournament bowls match compared with rest or a sedentary job is likely to be in the region of 350 calories and figurings show how diet can meet this energy demand.

'He could meet the extra demand for calories in many ways: He could, for instance, eat either $1\frac{1}{2}$ oz. of butter or 3 oz. of sugar or 2 oz. of sweet biscuits or 5 oz. of white bread or potato-chips or $3\frac{1}{2}$ oz. of mixed fruit pudding. He could also derive the same number of calories from either 18 oz. of fresh whole milk or about 3 oz. of Cheddar cheese or 5 oz. of fried eggs or 4 oz. of grilled beef steak or $3\frac{1}{2}$ oz. of fried pork sausages or 6 oz. of fried cod. He could also obtain 350 calories by drinking 39 oz. of bitter draught ale.'

There are a few guiding principles which would help him in the choice of food. Fortunately, he does not need to eat the equivalent of an additional 350 calories in one of his usual meals, because this is a significant increase on a normal meal and it might cause discomfort on the green.

The man in need of extra energy can increase the amount of food eaten at each meal and so spread the extra consumption throughout the day. He could eat extra snacks, an extra full meal at some convenient time during the day or substitute a full meal for the morning or afternoon cup of tea. For many people this is not convenient, so extra energy rich drinks, which are easy to make and quickly swallowed are often employed. For this purpose pure sugar or glucose can be used, but if so it should be remembered that these do not provide any nutrients, apart from energy, and if taken in the required amount may lead to temporary stomach discomfort. On the other hand sugars are said to be useful in that they are very quickly absorbed and utilized. There are proprietary mixtures, which are more pleasant to taste, which do provide extra nutrients and can be consumed as drinks to give rapidly assimilable energy.

Water and Salt Requirements

Body water constitutes approximately two-thirds of the body weight. A man weighing 65 kilograms (144 lb.) would contain about 40 litres (9 gallons) of water. The maintenance of water balance in the body is as important a criterion as any other for good health. In addition to the water output from the kidneys an appreciable volume of water is lost from the skin by sweating. The latter loss can be considerable during strenuous exercise.

Amongst other water soluble substances which are excreted through the skin, sodium chloride (common salt) is of significance. Under conditions of excessive sweating correspondingly large quantities of salt can be lost from the body. Lack of salt can lead to muscular cramp. The requirement of common salt would therefore be larger.

To summarize, one would suggest that a player should enjoy a varied diet, use his appetite and thirst as a guide to the amount to eat, and so take extra snacks or drinks as needed. He should make sure that he does take some salt and normally he will find it more comfortable and convenient to satisfy his appetite by frequent snacks, or energy-rich but readily digestible foods, rather than by a few heavy meals. There is a great tradition of 'steaks for strength' in Britain and few would argue against the general theory.

Yet it is undoubtedly true that many men and women find difficulty in digesting heavy meat meals when they reach middle-age. This tendency is often accentuated when the meal is taken before a period of nervous tension, i.e. before an important bowls match. I am indebted to Leonard Denham, Dip.M., M.Inst.M., for the following paragraphs concerning liquid meals for athletes, and serious bowlers should consider themselves in very much the same vein as other athletes. Mr. Denham writes:

'The problems of feeding athletes is probably as old as athletics itself. Much has been written on this subject yet many athletes still resort to ill-considered diets and the use of unnecessary supplements. Bullen *et al.* (1959)[1] state, "For centuries trainers and coaches have advocated special dietary schemes, stemming from older traditions and superstitions, and based on the belief that the ingestion of particular foods would augment the physical capacity or efficiency of the performer."

'Cooper *et al.* (1962)[2] say that so-called "health foods" are commonly used by trackmen and swimmers in the mistaken belief that one or two "wonder" ingredients will enable the athlete to perform beyond his normal capability. Even when a tram training table is maintained, there is a tendency to follow tradition rather than modern nutritional knowledge in arranging menus and feeding hours.

'Various authors have recommended pre-game diets based on the knowledge that under normal conditions digestion and absorption of a solid meal takes place within four hours. However, under stress this process is prolonged and Rose *et al.* (1963)[3] report a study of gastric motility in the pre-game situation on four football team members, "All of them had a decided gastric retention at $2\frac{1}{2}$ hours. After the game (from $6\frac{1}{2}$ to $7\frac{1}{2}$ hours after eating) there was still a considerable portion of the meal in the terminal jejunum and ileum. In other words, this meal was being digested and absorbed during the football game. It is a well-accepted theory that digestion or muscular activity or both are

[1] *American Journal of Surgery*, September 1959.
[2] *Journal of the Oklahoma State Medical Association*, December 1962.
[3] *Journal of the National Athletic Trainers Association*, November 1963.

compromised under such conditions. . . . Based on the know-ledge that solid food must be rendered liquid or semi-liquid before it is evacuated from the stomach, it was suggested that a high calorie liquid meal, such as that used in post-surgical cases, might be the answer to this problem. These liquid diets are highly nutritional, well balanced, and are readily digested and absorbed."

'Another complication of feeding athletes is their predisposi-tion to nausea and vomiting under stress. This is a well-known problem and a liquid food is likely to be better tolerated and reduce this distressing syndrome. In another report, Rose and his colleagues (1961)[1] commented on the delay in digestion of solid foods and went on to say, "On the other hand the liquid pre-game meal left the stomach very rapidly. Strength and en-durance of athletes seemed to be improved during the game. Nausea, vomiting and cramp were completely eliminated." Morton (1968)[2] states, "The practice of eating large quantities of meat, particularly in the pre-game meal, and the belief that it is helpful to the athlete is contrary to scientific evidence."

'In an effort to find out what sort of food would provide maximum blood-sugar levels in the shortest time, Professor Morton gathered together 60 physical education undergraduates at the Narrabeen Fitness Camp, Sydney, Australia. Half the group were put on a traditional steak meal (8 oz. steak, 3 oz. potatoes, 2 oz. pumpkin, 3 oz. peas) and the other half on a liquid meal.

'The experiment proved that the blood-sugar level was con-siderably higher among those who had consumed the liquid meal. It also provided that its peak was reached in much less time than it took for the steak meal to give full benefit. "It can be concluded that the ingestion of a high carbohydrate and low fat meal is followed by a more rapid and greater increase in blood sugar than after the steak meal," wrote Professor Morton.

[1] *Journal of the American Medical Association*, 7th October 1961.
[2] *Australian Journal of Sports Medicine*, July 1968.

'Liquid meals are clearly not the panacea for all dietary problems and are not the "open-sesame" to sensational improvement in performance. They do, however, reduce digestive problems in the pre-match stress situation and provide a rapid, balanced source of energy. Nutrament, a liquid food recently made available in this country in three flavours, provides 400 calories in each 13 fluid ounce can, which contains 50 grams of carbohydrate and 20 grams of protein. It also contains balanced amounts of vitamins and essential minerals so that unless an athelete suffers from a diagnosed deficiency state supplementary vitamins and minerals are not needed. All of the studies mentioned in this article refer to the use of Nutrament or Sustagen (a similar product made by the same manufacturer but not available in the United Kingdom) when liquid food is mentioned.'

The obvious fact arising from this is that any bowler who suffers from indigestion, stomach discomfort, or muzzy eyesight when playing important matches should experiment with liquid diets before matches.

My observations of bowlers in World Championship, Commonwealth Games and National Championships fill me with many misgivings. True, a good diet cannot make anyone bowl better than his best, but a bad one, either in content or timing, can bring a bowler far down below his best.

Sound sleep is tremendously important, not only to competitive bowlers but to all who want sound health and tranquil nerves.

It is a complex subject which was covered with exceptional thoroughness by health expert Francis Thorne in the January 1965 issue of *World Bowls*. He wrote:

'We spend a third of our lives asleep, yet though much is known about the physical changes connected with this phenomenon, the sleep mechanism and the mental changes associated with it remain a mystery. Nature has kept this secret closely guarded.

'Nevertheless, some useful facts have been gleaned, so let us examine what is known about sleep.

'Sleep is a state of unconsciousness occurring at regular periods during which the body, especially the nervous system, is refreshed and rejuvenated.

'It is the most complete form of rest because most of the body organs take time off during sleep; only the digestive, breathing and circulatory systems continue to work, and these only at a reduced rate. Therefore, relaxation is more or less complete.

'When sleep comes upon one, sight and smell are the first senses to be lost; hearing and touch go more slowly—a loud noise or a push will waken most people.

'The faculty first affected is will-power—and it is the last to return—hence the difficulty in getting up when the alarm clock bids. Leaping straight out of bed is not a good thing anyway.

'It is better to muse for a bit and rise slowly, thereby allowing the blood-pressure to return to normal without strain. Reasoning and the association of ideas go after will-power, then memory and imagination.

'On the physical plane, blood-pressure drops, we generate less heat and energy, body temperature falls (and the blood supply to the brain becomes feeble), respiration is slower and deeper, the heart beats slower, the kidneys produce less urine, and the liver, less bile.

'The skin becomes flushed with blood—hence the need to have enough covering, to avoid chills.

'*The Stages of Sleep*. Contrary to the general belief the deepest period of sleep is the first 1–2 hours, after which sleep grows lighter to just below the threshold of consciousness, until the 4th-5th hour, when we once more relapse into deep sleep and relaxation for a while before progressing by stages to wakefulness.

'There are many theories about the cause of sleep. One is that the nervous impulses from the brain are blocked. Another postulates the idea of a toxin (a poison) being responsible through accumulating during the waking hours until it permeates and dulls the central nervous system in a similar way.

'Yet another is that toward the end of the day, especially after strenuous mental or physical exertion, our body cells and brain become deprived of oxygen, thus producing sleep.

'In fact, of the oxygen taken in over 24 hours, 67 per cent is taken during the 12 hours of day, and 33 per cent during the 12 hours of night—so there may be something in this theory.

'The latest idea is that inhibition, always present in the brain, spreads over the body during sleep rather like night ousting day and that preliminaries connected therewith condition the brain for sleep and aid the inhibitory process.

'Tenable as some of these ideas seem, they are but theories— the exact mechanism of sleep remains a mystery.

'*How Much Sleep?* The amount we need depends on occupation, age and perhaps on sex, though the authorities seem to differ on whether men need more sleep than women.

'Some people can get by on a succession of "cat naps". Some need only a few hours daily, others are "whacked" without 8–10 hours.

'There are, of course, individual variations, and habit plays its part. It can be said, however, that brain workers need more sleep than those engaged in manual labour, and the young certainly need more than the old.

'A child of four requires about 13 hours, young children about 12 hours and until fifteen, 10 hours, thereafter reducing until 8 hours at nineteen.

'As a general rule for adults, the average of 8 hours holds good. Old people need less.

'If you lose much sleep you will soon show signs of it. Prolonged deprivation of sleep will reduce a man to a parlous state. The usual symptoms are lack of concentration, irritability and fatigue. The eyes become heavy lidded and sore, and there may be loss of appetite.

'These symptoms cause anxiety which, in turn, affects sleep and so the vicious circle goes on until broken by treatment.

'It has been stated that the loss of one night's sleep can be detected for a week. On the other hand, it is reported that a man who stayed awake for 230 hours (under drugs) was fresh again after only 11 hours sleep.

'An experiment conducted to see how long people could stay awake voluntarily showed 115 hours as the highest reading.

'Generally, Nature sees that sleep intervenes before any permanent harm is done, and most sleep deficits are made up during one good night's sleep. This leads to the question of insomnia.

'*Planning for Sleep:* Highly strung and emotional people are more prone to sleeplessness than the placid types, and the commonest causes are idleness during the day, mental stimulation at night, excitement and fear of insomnia.

'A hot drink/or a warm bath before retiring, light reading in bed—a combination of these will often induce sleep. But where the condition is obstinate a doctor should be consulted.

'A little planning in the bedroom can do much to lessen the chance of sleepness nights.

'There must be adequate ventilation. During the day leave the window open to clear away "bedroom fug". At night, leave one window open at least.

'Add another blanket to the bed rather than close the window. Do not, however, overload the bed with blankets. This is a common cause of restless sleep.

'A hard mattress is preferable to a soft one; most interior sprung ones of modern design are suitable. But avoid the feather bed like the plague. This encourages defects in posture.

'See that the bed is placed away from draughts, and that the reading lamp gives a good light, and is in a convenient position. Craning the neck to catch the light won't help to induce sleep.

'Quiet is essential but some people find a mild rhythmic noise, like the tick of a clock, soothing.

'Perhaps the most important thing is to establish a sleep rhythm. This means adhering to set routine. Prepare for, and go to bed at, the same time each night.

'This conditions the mind and body for sleep and established the rhythm. Late nights break it.

'Do not attempt mental gymnastics before retiring, nor engage in heated discussion.

'The best guarantee of sound sleep is a pleasantly tired body and a quiet mind.'

How many times have you heard tired bowlers complain 'oh my poor feet'? Certainly Francis Thorne is familiar with it and so he made a valuable contribution to *World Bowls* some years ago on this vital topic under the heading 'Oh, my poor feet!' It read:

'In all probability, this cry is heard periodically in households throughout the country. Yet the feet which are possibly the most hard-worked members of the body, are also the most neglected. People will buy expensive creams and lotions to keep their hands in good condition, but very few people will give more than a passing thought to the welfare of their feet. A housewife walks 8 to 10 miles a day doing her "chores", and in addition, has to stand for lengthy periods at the sink, whilst cooking, when in queues and so on. A bus conductor certainly will not cover less ground, and most of us cover a surprising distance every day.

'The feet are the platform for the body, and also serve as levers to propel the body along. There are no spare parts for the 26 bones of the foot; you have, in fact, only one pair of feet, which have to last a lifetime and, therefore, it would not seem out of place to give them some help in achieving this with the minimum of trouble. Incidentally, it is interesting that in the A.T.S., over 40 per cent of the recruits had defective feet, 25 per cent serious enough to necessitate immediate treatment.

'It has been said that men and women are as old as their feet make them, and most certainly "bad feet" can cause serious incapacity and reduction in efficiency, quite apart from the great inconvenience and pain. Very often "bad feet" will lead to malposture, and this in turn to disagreeable afflictions such as backache and protruding abdomen, to name but two. Foot health is, therefore, of prime importance. Here are a few rules to help your feet keep on walking painlessly.

'First of all, the feet must be clean. They should be washed each day, but not soaked for lengthy periods; they should be dried thoroughly especially between the toes, and talcum powder lightly dusted on. The nails should be trimmed and cut straight across and short. Do not push the cuticles down the side of the toe.

'Shoes are worn for protection and warmth, and as we spend about two-thirds of our lives in them, it is essential that they should be trouble-free. The prime rule is—shoes must fit, for foot trouble is caused by ill-fitting or badly made shoes. Women, more so than men, are slaves to footwear fashions which predispose to foot ailments. Here are some points to remember concerning shoes:

1. They should be long enough to allow ample space between the end of the toes and the end of the shoe, when standing up or walking.
2. They should be wide enough not to pinch, and when buying new shoes fit both feet. Incidentally, size numbers mean very little, as there is at the present no standardization on shoes. If you have bought a pair of 9's at one shop, you may not need 9's if you later patronize another. These sizes are a rough guide.
3. See that shoes fit snugly at the heel to give adequate support, and if you are wearing boots, make sure that there is some sort of ventilation in the leather.

'Heel height is important. There is a great deal of argument about this but men's shoes are fairly sensibly designed in this respect. What height of heel you can wear if you are a woman depends on what sort of foot you have. If you have a long, thin, bony type of foot, then for comfort you should avoid high heels, even 2 in. may be uncomfortable to this type of foot. In any case, such feet look silly in very high heels. If you have a high instep, you can almost certainly wear high heels in comfort. For work, particularly if you are standing, and for walking, low heels are ideal.

'It is important to keep the heels of your shoes made up level. If you walk heavily on one part of the heel and allow this to wear down a great deal, you can throw the foot out of position. This will affect the ankle, which will in turn affect the whole of your body posture. Along with shoes, we must consider hose.

'Stockings or socks which are too short can cause as much harm as short shoes; in fact it is now thought that ill-fitting hose may encourage the formation of bunions. It is a good rule always to wear hose when walking; the insides of shoes are never washed and are, therefore, a good home for bacteria. If you go without hose and develop a blister which bursts, keep it covered, as it may otherwise turn septic. It is a good thing to ring the changes on shoes, and not wear the same pair for too long a time. At the end of the day, place shoe-trees in your shoes to keep them in shape, and before putting on another pair let your feet rest awhile, wriggling the toes and generally giving them a little light relief.

'Following on last month's article, it is now relevant to consider some of the ailments which affect the feet.

'Weak ankles are a common complaint and can be strengthened simply by these exercises.

1. Walking on the toes or heels.
2. Walking up and down stairs.
3. Bicycling.
4. Skipping.
5. Foot rolling in a complete circle in both directions.
6. Sitting, drawing with a pencil held in the toes.

'Performed regularly, these simple exercises will be immensely beneficial, but perhaps numbers 1, 5 and 6 should be performed in private to avoid a reputation for eccentricity!

'Another common foot ailment is bunions, which may be caused by tight fitting socks, ill-fitting or badly shaped shoes. Treatment should be carried out by a chiropodist, but thereafter, check on footwear with care.

'Blisters will not appear if the feet are carefully shod, but if they do, treat them with care, for, if neglected, they can give rise to quite uncomfortable repercussions. See that a blister is kept clean and covered, and if it does not clear up quickly, consult your doctor or chiropodist.

'Perspiring is a completely natural function, and of course, this occurs about the feet perhaps more than any other part of the body. If it becomes excessive and, therefore offensive, bathe the feet in an antiseptic lotion, dry thoroughly and then rub with methylated spirit; let this dry, then dust with good talcum powder to which boric acid powder (10 parts) has been added. Change the socks daily, if possible, and sprinkle a little talc into each fresh pair.

'Foot warts, technically known as *Verruca pedis*, is a condition thought to be caused by a virus, and it is infectious. The area of infection is extremely tender and painful, and this increases if pressure is applied. The most commonly affected parts are the underpads of the toes, and the front of the heel pad, but any part of the foot may be attacked. The wart varies in size from a pinhead to a penny! When this condition appears in a community such as a school or club, infection can spread rapidly via the floors of changing and shower rooms, swimming baths and the like, and it is, therefore, important to adopt protective measures. Swab the floors with an antiseptic, make use of a prophylactic footbath and use slippers. Treatment, which varies from freezing with carbon dioxide "snow" to scraping and paring under local anaesthetic should be carried out only by a qualified person, such as a chiropodist or medical practitioner.

'One more condition which must be mentioned, is *Tinea pedis*, or Athlete's Foot. This is common and very infectious. The method of spread is almost the same as in the case of foot warts, and similarly strict protective measures must be taken in a community if it is to be restricted. This condition may be likened to a sort of ringworm on the foot, in which the areas underneath the toes turn soggy and white, with later peeling of the skin which reveals raw and painful areas.

'Spontaneous cure is exceptional and if a long period of discomfort and inconvenience is to be avoided, treatment must be prompt and vigorous. Bathe the feet in an antiseptic solution, and apply dressings of potassium permanganate (1 in 4,000) and give the feet as much rest as possible. Once the blistering stage is over, apply a calamine solution to dry up the affected areas, and to relieve itching. Then, night and morning, vigorously rub in Whitfields Ointment which you can obtain from your chemist at moderate cost. Wash the feet before each treatment.

'*Tinea pedis* is a condition which frequently returns, and so to minimize the chances of re-infection, keep the toe nails clean and trimmed. Disinfect shoes and socks by using formalin. The chemist who sells you this will also instruct you in its use.

'Finally, prevention is better than cure. The following rules will help you to avoid foot troubles:
1. Keep the feet clean.
2. Do not wear ill-fitting shoes.
3. Make sure that your shoes or socks are not too tight, so cramping the toes.
4. Do not neglect blisters, loose skin, etc.
5. When your feet are tired, bathe and rest them and change your socks frequently.
6. Visit a chiropodist twice a year. It is a fine form of insurance.'

Most bowlers like their pint of beer or tot of whisky. Many also smoke, cigarettes mostly, pipes quite a lot, cigars more rarely.

The dangers of smoking have been so thoroughly covered in newspapers and magazines that nothing much need be added here. Some men claim that an occasional cigarette helps calm their nerves and it would be presumptous of me to challenge such beliefs. Maybe for an established smoker to give up completely would impose too great a hardship on him. Yet who can ignore the evidence piling up in damnation of smoking? So the only reasonable advice I can offer is that it is better and safer not to smoke and if you must, well then, in considerable moderation.

If you do decide to give it up completely, do not become an avid sweets eater for nothing puts on weight more quickly than an excess of sugary sweets. A few fruit drops will not cause great harm, chewing-gum less, though I must confess here to a personal and probably unreasonable aversion to the sight of a regularly champing jaw.

Alcohol is another question. Like anything else, taken to excess it is harmful but in moderation it does not hurt and can, indeed, bring positive benefits.

Frequently bowlers hurry from work to play their county and other competitions. Often a long journey is entailed, followed by a hurried sandwich before the match begins. Naturally placid players may be able to tolerate this without undue suffering but most of us suffer nervous wear—maybe subconsciously—in such situations. Here, contrary to general opinion, I believe that, if it is possible, a small glass of sherry followed by five minutes with feet up and then a light sandwich may help to lessen tension and to bring a little sustenance to a player. Once on the green he may beneficially suck a Dextrosol tablet or take Glucodin every couple of ends. Glucose cannot give you more stamina than you possess naturally but it can help burn up lactic acid and so eke out that stamina longer.

However, limit the pre-match pick-me-up to one glass. A bloated, over-weighted stomach and slightly bleary eye cannot possibly help accuracy, consistency, or endurance. Furthermore, as you will learn later, a slight degree of tension and nervousness is almost certainly necessary to tiptop competitive effectiveness.

Stiffness is an occupational hazard so far as bowlers are concerned. The answer is a warm to hot bath followed by massage, using a mild embrocation. Research has shown that massage restores muscle effectiveness very quickly though if those muscles are immediately thrown back into intense effort the after effects are severer than if they had been left alone.

Bowls cannot seriously be deemed strenuous, in the sense that soccer, rugby, or tennis are strenuous. So massage can be recommended almost without reservation, especially at the end of a day of match play.

Massage stimulates blood circulation, the blood carrying oxygen that burns up acid. But at such times one is vulnerable to draughts and care should be taken to protect those muscles that have been massaged.

This brings me to the subject of clothing and the advisability of wearing absorbent material so that there is no chance of sweat remaining on the body, there to be dried by the wind. That is the quick way to collect fibrositis, a painful rheumatic condition caused by inflammation of fibrous tissues. So, apart from wearing comfortable, absorbent clothing, always carry a sweater to don the moment play ends or when you feel the slightest traces of coldness. Fibrositis is unhappily simple to collect and, apart from being painful, is as useful to smooth movement as thick rust is to a hinge. And can anyone imagine smooth, regular deliveries from a bowler whose every movement brings restricting twinges of severe pain?

Geoff Kelly, a gold medallist in the World Championships at Kyeemagh, walked five miles three nights a week as training. He is an ultra keen competitor but he does win championships. As a generalization, walking plus a few gentle exercises at home each morning or evening plus a diet based on the recommendations in this chapter, sufficient sleep, and reasonable care of the feet is all that an ambitious bowler should find necessary.

One final word on training. Do not neglect creaking or aching joints, especially the knees. No less than the shoulder, the knees are vital in delivery. They must bend and move with the smoothness of a beautifully machined jet engine. Any catchings or twinges will destroy the regular step forward and perfect control vital to accuracy and direction. Remember that prevention is better than cure and at the slightest sign of stiffness or pain, take immediate action. Massage at the first possible moment. Do not drop into bed telling yourself 'it will have gone in the morning'. No matter how tired you may be, run that bath and flop in it. Massage some Algipan or similar embrocation into the joint and relax in your bed.

Rain and cold take a heavy toll of middle-aged and elderly muscles so treat yourself to a sound set of waterproof clothing; a loose fitting macintosh and tweed cap is not good enough. Keep warm and as dry as you can.

Apart from helping your bowls, these simple and reasonably elementary rules can make everyday life just that bit more zestful and enjoyable.

4

How Practice Makes Perfect

There are many players who derive as much pleasure from practising as they do from actual participation in competitive matches. This is splendid because one must never forget that the primary social purposes of bowls are recreation and the provision of exercise.

Let me here interject that there is now evidence suggesting that a man who exercises throughout his life increases his chances of longevity and certainly prolongs his active life.

However, in the minds of most people, the object of practice is improvement, and this is the context which must be studied.

What happens when one practises a shot which needs strengthening in order to withstand the psychological pressures likely to be met in competition?

The first point to emphasize is that it is just as easy to practise and become grooved in a faulty technique as it is in one which is sound. Once the grooving has been established, two problems have to be solved—ungrooving or unlearning the faulty technique, followed by learning the correct one.

It is as well, perhaps, to understand how grooving takes place and this I cover in another section of this chapter dealing with mental rehearsal. Sufficient here to record that when the brain 'instructs' a muscle or set of muscles to perform a series of movements, it does so with a stream of electrical impulses.

Each repetition of the movements eases very slightly the fol-

lowing passage of nerve impulses—burns a pathway as it were—
and the difficulty of eliminating that neural 'pathway' and sub-
stituting another logically increases the more it is 'burned' into
the system.

Convinced, I hope, of the dangers of unsupervised or unthinking traditional methods of practice, you should be willing to
delve yet a little deeper into the psychology of learning.

Learning derives from remembering but there is a vital fact of
this which is known in psychology by the rather clumsy title reminiscence. To understand this better, imagine an experiment.
It is an experiment which has been repeated many times and the
results measured under strict laboratory conditions.

The subject is set a physical skills task unlike anything he has
ever before met. His performance at the task can be measured or
counted precisely. He is put to work, note made of his progress
and when he becomes tired—say after seven or eight minutes—
he is stopped and made to relax in conditions which do not per-
mit him to think unduly about what he has been doing.

After ten minutes or so he is returned to the task and something rather unexpected is discovered. Instead of resuming with
a degree of skill similar or a little below that at which he stopped,
the subject will often show a distinct improvement. Indeed, if he
had begun the task in a highly motivated state of determination
to succeed, his post-rest improvement over pre-rest performance
may be quite staggering.

The theory underlying this strange phenomenon necessitates
a distinction between performance (i.e. actually performing the
task) and habit (i.e. the organization of the central nervous
system so that the task can be performed).

It should be clear that no matter how skilfully the task can be
performed, it won't be performed at all unless the subject decides
to do so.

In mathematical terms, then

$$\text{Performance} = \text{Habit} \times \text{Drive}$$

However, once the task is begun it seems that a further nervous reaction takes place—rather skin to the increase of resis-

tance to an electric current in a wire as the temperature of that wire rises—which gradually inhibits the action.

This reaction is known as reactive inhibition and it is thought by psychologists to be the objective reality which lies behind boredom and also behind fatigue in those tasks where the work load is fully covered by aerobic capacity.

This reactive inhibition works against inner drive, first spoiling performance and, when its total equals drive, bringing the performance to an end.

Sometimes this stop will be conscious and voluntary, but often the subject will pause momentarily without even realizing it himself.

This has been proved by tests in which the performing subject has been charted on an electro-encephalogram. This 'brain message' measuring machine shows patterns during poor performance and momentary pauses which are identical with those produced during sleep. Here, perhaps, is the reason for so many missed sitters and, maybe, for some motor-car accidents.

Now, the greater the motivation, the greater the reactive inhibition, but the quicker it dispels with rest and the greater is the jump forward in post-rest performance. Thus are shown the importance of motivation and the importance of correctly phasing a practice session.

On the whole, introverts tend to produce reactive inhibition more slowly than extroverts and so are more liable to show 'stick-at-it-iveness'.

How, then, can this be translated into a practical plan for on-green training? Each man and woman must discover his or her optimum work-relax cycle, but when seriously intending to develop one particular shot or movement I would suggest eight to ten minutes purposeful application should generate a 'waking-sleep' degree of reactive inhibition and that a complete rest should then be taken from that shot. After ten minutes of rest, reminiscence will result in a step forward—if the technique of the shot is good. Remember, one can equally strongly groove a poor shot.

Rest may be obtained by switching to some other facet of the game, for example, for backhand to forehand, but I consider it should be to something a little gayer than shot development, say ten minutes of firing. After all, one should derive happiness from playing, both from a sociological aspect and from the motivational angle. A normal person wishes to continue and improve when he is enjoying himself. Indeed, I rate happiness from playing as the strongest motivator of all.

The attentive reader may now be wondering how this relates to the long hours of practice indulged in by men like David Bryant or Percy Baker who are undoubtedly among the most successful bowlers in history.

It must be understood that there are two types of reactive inhibition, perceptual and muscular. Perceptual applies where the brain is being used as a 'translator' of ideas into actions, e.g. when learning a new shot or grooving an old one.

Muscular reactive inhibition occurs when the perceptual part has virtually ceased, i.e. when a shot has become fully grooved and completely automatic.

It is far slower developing than perceptual reactive inhibition.

To make things crystal clear, when striving to develop a 'grooved' or 'regrooved' shot you should work in relatively short, go-stop phases as this speeds learning considerably.

Once the action becomes completely automatic lengthen the 'go' phases. After all, one cannot stop to allow inhibition to dispel in the middle of a match.

One can, however, relax and take ample time between ends, though in advocating an 'on-and-off' system of concentration I am treading on very dangerous grounds. Nevertheless, one of the notable features about so many champions is an instinctive ability to 'pace' their matches correctly.

This truly is an instinct because I doubt if more than a handful of players in the world know the theory which lies behind this. Now, at least, readers should be able to apply intellectually knowledge they lacked instinctively.

Phased practice demands self-discipline and intense will to

succeed; it is so much easier to deliver a few forehand and backhand draw shots and then enjoy a couple of hours play while indulging in the self-delusion that this is good match practice.

It is impossible to overstress the major part mental discipline plays in improvement and I make no apology for returning to the point in discussing another valuable way in which it can help the grooving of shots or methods. It is particularly applicable to people with limited chances of winter practice.

But first the reiteration of a general principle of learning which is so logical that most people know it instinctively.

Put in its broadest sense and with, perhaps, too much simplification, this says that if—to use figures instead of symbols—a total of 24 hours is available for learning a skill, say a backhand delivery, the end result from 48 daily sessions each lasting $\frac{1}{2}$ hour will be better than from 3 daily sessions each of 8 hours duration.

Undoubtedly there is a point of optimum balance between many short and a few long sessions but, as a general principle, numerous short sessions are better than a few long ones. Remember reactive inhibition.

Is there any scientific justification to support players' claims that the 'thinking sessions' helped their improvement?

Firstly, there is now abundant evidence that the passage of a nerve current through a chain of nerves—caused, perhaps, through the execution of a forehand draw shot—does not leave that chain of nerves unchanged.

The modification seemingly takes place primarily at the synapses; a synapse is the point of communication between two nerve cells. These are the points where the 'messages' are passed from one set of nerves to another and the modification which takes place simplifies the subsequent passages of similar 'messages'. In bowls language, 'grooving' slowly takes place. It is possible that this phenomenon is at the roots of all learning, conditioning and habit. Thus constant repetition of a movement gradually improves the efficiency of the nerves in repeating that movement—be it a good or bad movement.

But this refers to repetition of an actual movement, so how does it link up with imagining?

For this it is necessary to refer to some experiments carried out in America. In these experiments electrodes were attached to human 'guinea-pigs' and connected to very sensitive amplifiers which measured the 'nerve currents and patterns' when the 'guinea-pigs' performed specific movements.

The 'guinea-pigs' then had the particular limbs—sometimes it was their arms—fixed down and they were instructed to imagine themselves repeating their test movements. Remember, they could not move.

The 'nerve currents' produced by imagination tallied precisely with those recorded when the actual, physical movements were made.

It is, therefore, a logical deduction that 'grooving' of the neurons and synapses also took place.

Certainly this provides a scientific reason for the improvements noted in the cases cited by people in bowls and particularly by golfers.

Such 'mental grooving' is far from easy to achieve, for it requires considerable self-discipline to take oneself off to a quiet spot every day for, perhaps, fifteen minutes. Even greater self-discipline is needed actually to concentrate on mental stroking for that period.

In order to test the truth of this, put down the book, empty your mind of all thought and then try to keep your mind a complete blank for one minute. Stray thoughts will come stealing in after very few seconds and it will take a fair degree of control on your part not to follow one of these 'strays' in the first three-quarters of a minute. If you can keep your mind a blank for two minutes you should be sufficiently disciplined mentally to stand a promising chance of using 'mental grooving' to advantage.

There is, of course, a limit to the amount of improvement that can be achieved in this way. Nevertheless a great deal can be achieved in the mind alone, especially in terms of learning new shots or even in mastering new methods of placement.

No less important, it is valuable as an exercise in objective concentration and mental self-discipline.

A word of warning. The laws of reactive inhibition still apply, so in 'mentally rehearsing' new grooving work in fairly short 'go-rest' phases.

I have now covered fairly thoroughly a theory which should allow any ordinary player to improve quickly and markedly—if he applies that theory correctly.

The foregoing covers fairly comprehensively the theory of learning and suggests a general policy for practice. Recommending specifics is difficult, for each man is going to have one set of special requirements this week, another next month and so on.

For that reason I believe it is helpful for a bowler to seek out another equally keen to improve and then to work together with him. In this way A can watch B, spot his weaknesses and suggest practices while B can do the same for A.

Actually most practice is likely to be concerned with improving delivery techniques in order to gain greater accuracy of land and length. David Bryant advocates the mastery of direction, believing an 'in-line' bowl, be it behind or in front of the jack, to be of greater potentiality than one to the side. So he practises direction by delivering his bowls over handkerchiefs spread on the green. It is a simple system and one which has proved itself to the hilt as far as he is concerned.

In seeking improvement in direction Bryant worked on his delivery technique and in so doing achieved a rhythmic flow which no one has exceeded and few, if any, equalled.

A short while ago I wrote, 'The delivery must be capable of sending bowl after bowl along a precise, desired line. How this is achieved must be left to each individual reader.'

Those words were read by Kenneth B. Okell, a scientifically minded Essex bowler in whom they struck a sympathetic chord. He described what had happened in an article in the March 1970 issue of *World Bowls* which I repeat here:

73

'These words were probably written about 1966. In November 1969 the book was read by a keen but far from competent bowler who, by a coincidence, undertook in 1966 some solo practice to achieve a particular objective, but subsequently discovered accidentally how to send his bowls along a precise, desired line.

'In my occupation of manufacturing engineering one understood exact dimensions, exact limits being stated to plus or minus × ten thousandth parts of an inch. But in my new world of bowls and all its manifold skills I listened to weird and abstract terms of "measurement", e.g. "a yard off", "a pound on", "more green", "less green", "a running wood", "a dying shot" and many other utterances.

'I asked questions as to how to achieve the skip's requests and on the occasions I got a reply, invariably it was that "it comes with experience". But it did not come in the first three seasons.

'During this period, playing at No. 2, the opportunity was taken to try out various makes and sizes of bowls—opinions and advice on this was diligently sought. But the answers did not appear to be forthcoming and by the end of the 1965 season I realized I was in a rut, but still liked bowls immensely.

'In April 1966 I bought a new set of Henselite Championship bowls. Size $5\frac{1}{16}$ in. was selected because my stature of six feet and fourteen stone could easily propel it. Printed on the box 3 lb. $5\frac{7}{16}$ oz.—mahogany—and made in Australia.

'That was the complete information made available to me about the bowls. I had still less about my own characteristics.

'Consideration was given as to how some method or analytical exercise could be devised to determine exactly how the bowls would perform on a bowling green; how could I possibly select the "correct green" in a game until I knew how the bowls would perform at various lengths of shot?

'So along to the club green, but with no preconceived ideas of my method. After a few roll-ups a thought came—practise sending the bowls along the rink dividing string to ascertain how much they curved from the string.

'In this exercise I got the first of many surprises to follow. It was difficult to despatch the bowl from the hand accurately along the side of the string and the thought occurred of what happened in a normal game.

'This practice along the dividing string appealed, so a ball of thinnest white twine, four 2 in. nails, and a piece of hardboard 24 in. × 4 in. to wind the twine on to were acquired.

'Before the second practice session I asked the head groundsman, Syd Alleeson, who personally tends the green, for his permission to set down some twine for practice and he readily agreed.

'The Ford club green at Ilford, Essex, was laid in 1959. It is maximum size of hard structure Cumberland turf, very free running, London and Southern Counties B.A. and Essex County B.A. approved, and used by those associations. It can take a tremendous amount of rain with only a very slight effect on its surface.

'Resuming the practice, the white twine was laid down the centre line of the rink using a 2 in. nail pushed under the bottom of the turf (Fig. 12/1). The difficulty of sending the bowl along the twine persisted so the mat was moved about 6 in. to the left-hand side.

'Additionally, the stepping-off-the-mat delivery method was discarded and a static position of delivery was tried out and developed with appreciable improvement in results (Fig. 12/2).

'During these sessions no jack was used, only the forehand played, and the same procedure adopted when playing the reverse way.

'Notes were scribbled on a pad. After four sessions of about two-and-a-half hours, each spread over some weeks, I knew exactly how the bowls would curve and bend from the twine line at various lengths and strengths of despatch. The variation was considerable. It surprised me.

'During this practice the bowls' stopping positions formed a scattered pattern so a second twine was set down (Fig. 12/3). The far end nail of the rink dividing string was utilized and the twine taken to the C/L nail at mat end.

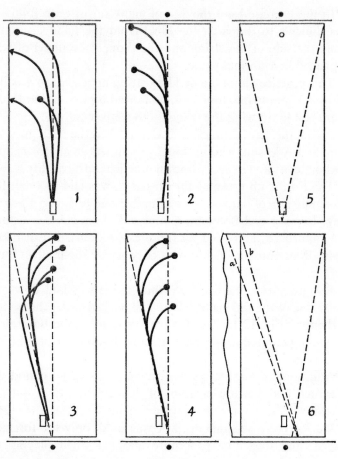

Fig. 12.

'Practising sending bowls along the angled twine using back-hand soon indicated that this was the approximate line of direction for the bowls to stop near the C/L of the rink when using full length delivery. When bowling the reverse way the twines were a distraction but soon overlooked as I set myself to visually fix the line of direction.

'Now I was keen to find out what would happen on other lengths of shot. Still using the identical twines and mat positions,

76

two weeks later came another surprise to find that if, irrespective of length of shot, I laid the bowl accurately along the angled twine, it would stop on or within six inches either side of the C/L of the rink (Fig. 12/4).

'This was pleasing and for many following practice sessions I kept to this specialized drill. Also, I began to think that the particular objective I had set out to ascertain had been realized.

'It will be noted in Fig. 12/2, 3, 4, that the side of the mat had been offset about 6 in. from C/L of rink for the reason stated earlier. Although I did not know it at this time, it had reached the end of its initial usefulness, but more will be heard of offset later.

'By now, the middle of the 1968 summer season, I had gained a place as lead in the club four-rink team. Even so, in major events and club fixtures too many bad bowls were delivered, particularly narrow shots. So there was more thinking and reference to notes scribbled during practice sessions.

'Something fundamental had got to be ferreted out in practice —something that had not yet been found out in six seasons of club fixtures.

'The task was this: Knowing exactly how the bowls would perform at all lengths of shot when despatched along a specific line, I now had to find out where that line was on the rink from the basic mat position. So the twines were set from the far end corner pegs, and under the mat to the C/L of the rink at the mat end, and the jack was used in practice for the first time (Fig. 12/5).

'Accuracy of length had got to be of minor importance. The practice objective was to get the bowls to finish on the C/L of the rink.

'With the mat in its basic position it was now necessary to move the twines to find the task objective line. This generated the thought of *where to or where from*. Pondering on this, I found it logical to use the rink corner pegs as a base from which to measure and record any redispositions of the twines, affording as they did checks at each end of the rink.

'I became an addict of the corner pegs. The Laws stipulate

four corner pegs painted white on the banks of the rink. They are not subject to change due to variation of light, shadows, or rain, and are rarely obscured by persons on the green.

'They are a valuable fixed asset. It seems a paradox that the rink dividing strings must be green yet the corner pegs have to be white.

'My researches soon had the twines on the move as a result of observing the paths and stop positions of the bowls delivered to maximum length jack. The twines at the mat end only needed redisposition.

'Some cross checks of shifting the twines at the jack end proved negative. The backhand was ironed out first then the forehand. The ability to despatch a bowl along a line from the moment of separation from the hand had attained proficiency, but a number went adrift and were disregarded because at the moment of separation their direction was seen to be wrong. It is my belief that only twine guides can clearly, accurately, and instantly signal this almost micrometer-scale information.'

Much could be recounted about the happenings in this objective line practice, but detail is tedious and the adage 'One man's meat . . .' is respected.

'Fig. 12/6 shows the pattern of the objective lines of my delivery. These emerged after five practice sessions of about two-and-a-half hours each, including bowling the reverse way using visual sighting direction only.

'This was not the non-stop procession it sounds. Alterations of the twines is time consuming—not the shifting but the thinking and checking. The hours pass too quickly.

'An interesting feature is the degree by which the twine guides became offset from the mat as compared with the original "convenience" settings in Fig. 12/2, 3, 4. Some sly things were done with the mat during the practice—there were no umpires about.

'In Fig. 12/3, 4 and 5 the mat was pivoted about in all directions to find out anything about positioning the body and feet in relation to the line of despatch of the bowl, but no single feature was detected at this stage.

'Mention should be made of the luck enjoyed during 1969 practice. The superb weather from the end of May onwards and corresponding condition of bowling green provided almost laboratory conditions for the experiments.

'A naughty fault still lurked about in practice and games, i.e. occasional narrow shots on the backhand, so a third twine was set on the rink. Fig. 12/6 line "B" is the objective line already established and used. It was from this line that the naughty fault used to occur.

'The third twine is line "A" set about two to three feet to L.H. side of far corner peg then down to mat end and tied to nail of line "B". Numerous bowls in runs of four were sent down both lines alternately.

'It then happened that a badly-laid bowl inside line "A" came to stop on C/L of rink. Deliberately about a dozen bowls were sent along the same "badly laid" line and all stopped near the rink C/L.

'About two dozen more bowls were sent down each line this time alternating in singles. Soon the answer became known—it was the positioning of the body on the mat. The body had to face outwards along the "A" line but the sighting and delivery had to be along the "B" line to counteract some inherent personal characteristic in the delivery action.

'This experience caused me to be more careful than hitherto in positioning the feet and body on the mat. In the previous years of bowling I had no idea that the backhand had an inherent drift, wobble, swing, or some other defect. Whether it was body, legs, shoulder, arm, etc. was not found out.

'This discovery was accidental and there may be more to follow. But for the "messages" from the twines it is doubtful if it would have been revealed for it is a difficult, almost impossible mental exercise to retrace the exact path of a bowl along a rink, or to make a comparison of differently-directed bowls, particularly if the difference is small as in the case of lines "A" and "B".

'At the mat end both lines were secured to the same nail and at the point along the lines where the bowls started to curve in, the lines may have been about fifteen inches apart, but this is a guess as measuring was done at the corner pegs only.

'Purposely, many related matters about the delivery have not been mentioned because visits to Mortlake to watch the National Championships provide so much food for thought—for instance, the stoic-like, calm squat followed by the all-stations-in-action delivery of The Master, D. J. Bryant. Then the parade ground drill on the mat in slow motion of N. R. W. Groves who seemed to do everything except use a theodolite or a compass and, lastly, the catapult-cum-airborne-cum-advanced-gymnastics of J. Davidson, to mention a few extreme contrasts in techniques.

'But all had one thing in common—they delivered the bowl along a precise desired line more often than their opponent so as to win the coveted National Championships.

'Trial ends now have an enhanced value as compared with the previous use made of them. Length of the bowling green, width of rink, position of mat vary but corner peg sighting is considered to be more positive than other options for assessing the correct "green" to be used for various length shots.

'When throwing the jack, in addition to the length requested by the skip, care is exercised with direction. It is free extra practice enjoyed by the lead player only, yet about 95 per cent have to be centred. It is difficult to send even an ideal size and weight spherical ball along a precise, desired line.

'A fair question here would be: "What did all the practice reflect in terms of good or other shots in an average game?" Details were not recorded but a "shadow" standard exists for future comparisons.

'It was on page 7 in *World Bowls*, issue of May 1969, concerning the 16 players of the Paddington and Richmond clubs who earlier had contested the final of the Denny Cup indoor event. The statistical presentation of 192 shots observed was interesting inasmuch as the number of shots under the categories of "fair" and "poor" seemed a surprisingly high percentage of the total analysed.

'The twine guides will be used in the 1970 season. It is doubtful whether any other economic medium could perform similar functions as efficiently for, in addition to setting down a particular track or tracks on a rink to find, check, prove, or disprove some element, they also communicate the result of the mental intentions and related physical actions of a delivery as already stated—clearly, accurately, instantly.

'In retrospect it may be that the ground covered could be realigned to obtain the same results in shorter time. It was ironic that the naughty backhand defect was discovered in the last stages of all the exercises. Was it possible to have found it out earlier, was it an instance of "not seeing wood for trees", or was something amiss in priorities?

'Very many hours were expended with the twines, the pay off was handsome and was, in the language to be learned later in *The Watney Book of Bowls*,[1] the delivery capable of sending bowl after bowl along a precise, desired line.'

[1] *The Watney Book of Bowls* by C. M. Jones (Queen Anne Press, 1967).

5
Sighting

Difficult it may be to groove a smooth, rhythmic, regular delivery, yet this is possibly simpler than another, key factor which could be considered part of delivery, namely sighting for direction.

There are several schools of thought concerning this, one of which is, in effect, mechanical. In this system some mark which accords with the draw is used as a 'sighter' for the line. Maybe it is an object on the bank, a patch of darker or lighter grass on the green, a mark on the string bounding the rink, or. . . .

Maybe this is minimally permissible for a beginner under instruction but no bowler with match-winning ambitions should seriously consider adopting this system permanently. What happens when your opponent changes the mat position? Or the mark rubs off? Or is moved?

Far better to learn to 'feel' the arc of the bowl in one's stomach, to learn until they are burned into the brain the arcs of draw. This system can be helped to some degree by use of the string for it is, on each rink you bowl, fixed in position for the duration of your match.

In outdoor championship play the rink should, according to the rules, be 19 feet wide. That is approximately 9 feet from each side of the mat, assuming the mat is central. Now, clearly, the extent of a bowl's curve is governed by the pace of the green. The longer the bowl trickles, the more it will swing. However, each man's set of bowls possesses its own characteristics.

Hundreds of checks carried out under championship conditions have revealed to me that the average Henselite used on a 14 seconds green to draw to a jack 30 yards from the front of the mat will have to go out to the string for a dead draw. Please do not—repeat, do not—take this as an absolute figure. At Teesside recently I observed similar bowls of opposing players differing in draw by as much as a foot, or even more.

Yet the basic approach is right and any keen player motivated strongly for success can make use of this effectively through systematic, recorded practice over a period of time.

It entails going on to the same rink of the same green on a number of evenings, setting the jack at the same length always— say 30 yards from the front of the mat—and timing the start to stop run of a bowl to that jack. Remember that the bowl starts to curve perceptibly after travelling roughly three-fifths of the way up the green. How near—or far—to the string it has to go in order to return to dead centre at 30 yards can be assessed and entered in a book.

After a while a complete set of tables will emerge and this can be consulted as and when necessary. When playing a match the green can be timed while your opponent is bowling on the trial ends. So you can begin playing with a scientific knowledge of the amount of land to take and adjust this as and when necessary.

Many bowlers are careless in using their feet. This carelessness, incidentally, often spreads to their first and second deliveries on each end in singles. Even the best bowlers occasionally suffer from this and I recall quietly suggesting to John Scadgell, that great Commonwealth Games gold medallist skip, that he was becoming guilty of this. Some years later, when taking part in a *World Bowls* magazine research, he was kind enough to record on his questionnaire that this was the finest piece of advice he had ever been given.

Returning to the topic of feet, the 'Basic Bowls' course book-let specifies that right-handed bowlers should point the right foot along the desired delivery line when using the forehand and the left foot when bowling on the backhand.

Some bowlers point the inside foot—for a right hander, the left foot for the forehand, the right for the backhand—at the jack, the heels being kept together. This system is advocated by R. T. Harrison, a successful Australian teacher and bowler.

On the other hand, Frank Soars, another prominent bowler and teacher from Australia, keeps his feet parallel when delivering; like Harrison, he places his left hand on his left knee for support.

So two eminent bowlers with enviable records correspond in all factors of delivery other than the inside foot. In terms of sighting, then, this evidence suggests the use of that foot is individual and not decisive.

More important to sighting and maintenance of good balance is the use of the whole of the left side—leg, body and arm. The line having been established, the inner leg must be under complete control, especially on the forehand because it moves in the case of athletic deliveries. That control of direction and balance.

If you decide to use the system of sighting suggested do remember the speed of a green often varies slightly from hour to hour, perhaps by as much as 2 seconds from early morning to 1.30 p.m. or thereabouts and then back 2 seconds as the afternoon draws on. The sun, too, has an effect on the nap because the grass follows the sun. So if the sun travels east to west across the green, the nap—when bowling towards the sun—in the morning in the Northern Hemisphere will be slightly forehand to backhand and then vice versa in the afternoon. It will be vice versa bowling with the sun behind you. The difference may not be great, perhaps half a second. Yet this will necessitate widening or narrowing the aiming point by about 6 inches to allow for either extra run with the nap or less run against it. Remember, in sighting the line is a constant irrespective of length of jack; it is the distance along it that varies with length of jack, as you have learned in an earlier chapter.

Whatever the system adopted, it is possible to develop reasonable control of direction by use of the brain; it is a technical attribute. This is less true of length because length comes from touch which is largely inborn. Nevertheless, like most other things, it can be improved through practice.

Human touch is most sensitive at the finger-tips so a bowler who rolls the bowl out of his fingers will, all other factors being equal, possess a superior sense of touch to that of a man who pushes the ball out of his palm.

This leads straight back to the Bryant theory of using over-size bowls.

There is one sound piece of advice which should be observed. It is to go out on the green with, if possible, eight bowls of identical weight, size and bias and set up three jacks at, say, 25, 30 and 35 yards. Try drawing to each in turn, bowl by bowl. Concentrate on all the finer facets of technique that you have learned. Treat each bowl as though the outcome of a big tournament depended on it.

Do not overdo this practice. At most, quarter of an hour's intensive practice should suffice and, at least, 10 minutes. Repeat the process on the next day—and the next—and the next. Do this for a summer and you will surprise yourself with the advance you make. Vary from forehand to backhand for a quarter of an hour spell each time. Do not alternate forehand and backhand bowl by bowl because you are trying to burn the sensation into your nerves. That is why concentration is so vital—you can as easily burn in a bad habit as a good one if the whole of your mind is not devoted to executing each tiny facet of every delivery precisely as desired.

This system of practice backed with regular match play, preferably with a skip who fully understands and endorses your objects, should enable you to develop a sound draw shot. This, one is always told, is the essence of good leading in a rink or triple.

A lead, so it is stated, has as his object doing better than his opposite number in a direct battle for shots. There are players who could be named who actually keep count of the number of ends on which they held shot when the leading finished.

Yet is this sufficient? In the 1958 British Empire and Commonwealth Games, the England skip John Scadgell discovered there were aspects of play in which he could outbowl his South African opposite number. His lead, Norman King, was significantly superior to the opposing lead on short jacks but only about equal on long jacks. However, Scadgell needed long jacks for his plan and so called upon King to sacrifice his personal superiority for the overall good.

This King did willingly and he praised Scadgell's tactics even though his own play that day was far from satisfying. The result? England beat South Africa to win the Gold Medal.

So what kind of a game did King have? Personally I have no doubts. He saw his job as lead was to bowl for the good of the four overall, not for personal satisfaction. He, therefore, had a very good game though I have yet to find a book which advocates this kind of approach to leading.

Leading is generally related to drawing but I recall the England-Canada fours match in the 1966 World Championships. On one end the England lead Cedric Smith drew his first bowl plumb on the jack. Without one second's hesitation the Canadian lead unleashed a fierce firing shot smack on target, crashing the jack out of bounds for a replay of the end.

Altogether that morning the Canadians forced 16 ends to be replayed, stinging one England player to say, 'That wasn't bowls, it was skittles.'

Whether or not his remark was justified is irrelevant. The title of this book is specific and the Canadians won that match. I believe that if they had adopted traditional tactics, they would have been outdrawn, outpositioned and beaten by England. Their aggressive methods disrupted the English four so who can denigrate the strong-arm tactics of their lead on the end in question? In fact, he fired on other ends with mixed results.

Leading, then, basically demands accurate drawing to the jack and some bowlers use the straightest running bowls they can find, their theory being that 'the shortest distance between A and B is a straight line'.

Since a strong case can be made for direction being more important than length—though not so valuable as perfect mastery of both—there could be wisdom in purchasing two straight running bowls for use exclusively when leading in fours play.

Yet why 'exclusively'? Why not for use as the first two bowls in singles, the other two being wider drawing bowls capable of curving their way round obstacles? True, it would necessitate considerable adaptability yet I believe that mastery could be achieved by scrupulous use of the practice theories and methods advocated earlier in this book.

In dealing with the number two let me immediately get out of the way one of his duties—keeping the score. Nowadays bowls matches are widely reported in local and provincial papers, often from scorecards. So if you please.

(1) Print the initial and name of every bowler.
(2) Where possible, add first names.
(3) Use a clear pencil or ball-point pen.
(4) Write clearly and keep the card dry.
(5) Hand it in to the club secretary or official in charge of the match or tournament.

Having disposed of that, consider now your duties as a bowler, Often these are described as complementary to the lead; he has failed to deliver his bowl close to the jack or has bowled short, wide or long. The number two must rectify the situation.

Often, however, the lead will have laid the foundation of a good head and the skip will ask for positional bowls entailing delivery not to a clear target like the jack or another bowl but to a blank space at the head.

This is a more difficult task than bowling to an object and a wise number two should always establish an understanding with the skip to indicate clearly the precise position he hopes the bowl will finish . . . and to keep his signal—a handkerchief maybe—steady at that spot for a sufficient time to let the distance fix itself in the wise number two's eye and mind.

On the whole, it seems bowlers tend to underestimate distance once a marker has been removed. So fix the position clearly in mind, perhaps through relating it to some specific object which is not too far away from the target spot.

Having established the spot, deliberately imagine your bowl running down the green and curving to a stop dead on target.

Such 'mental rehearsal' is a well-tried and tested psychological tool whose value is considerable and profitable.

It has often been written and spoken that a number two should never be short lest the head be blocked for the third man and skip. This, of course, is an extension of the philosophy of an aggressive lead; the onus of responsibility for scoring is left to the third man and, even more, the skip.

This was the policy followed by Abdul Kitchell in the 1970 Commonwealth Games at Balgreen and which won the Fours gold medal for Hong Kong. I reported in *World Bowls*: 'It was the skilled use of that essential quality (accuracy) which established their superiority. In particular, they adopted a positive system of playing for the jack or, if outpositioned at the start of any end, of opening up the head so that their third man and skip had room to score or save towards the completion of the end.'

Occasionally a number two may use a firing shot, more often a yard on shot but mostly his task will be to draw, either to a definite target bowl or to a desired spot.

He must cultivate sufficient control, technical and mental, to avoid bunching at the head. And, finally, like children, a good number two should be seen but not heard—so do not try to take over your skip's duties.

The third man in a four has a difficult role to fulfil, especially in representative matches at county or national level. That he has caught the eyes of the selectors testifies he is above average level and so is probably one of the best bowlers in his club. As such he will normally be shouldering all the responsibilities of a skip. Suddenly instead of giving orders he will be taking them. Even if he is the most tranquil man alive, there will be numerous occasions when he and his skip will see the head differently and so consider it should be tackled in two contrasting ways. Most skips wish to bear full responsibility at all times. A few possess less self-confidence and need the reassurance of the third man. A small number are highly skilled technicians but not so talented tactically.

The textbooks say the third man should be unobtrusive and give advice or guidance only when asked. Certainly he must never be obtrusive but that need not infer never dropping a gentle hint or suggestion. Or, more important, using a quiet word now and then to bolster his skip's confidence.

Research into war-time R.A.F. bomber crews revealed that loss of confidence by one member of a crew noticeably affected the performances of other crew members. So it is in bowls. Loss of confidence by one man sooner or later brings down the others. And when it comes to confidence, the skip must exude it. No one can help the skip in this more than the third man.

At the start of each end the leads have a little, personal drawing to the jack contest in which bowls 6 inches or so from the jack are liable to earn loud applause from the bank. The number twos, in traditional English bowling, fill in the gaps and, again, 6 inches from the target bowl or position is liable to be considered adequate.

By the time these four participants walk to the head, eight bowls will be positioned around the jack, so limiting room for manoeuvre. Thus two or three inches one way or the other is quite likely to prove decisive. Thus, accuracy is of prime importance, whether it be in drawing, firing or delivering bowls to run the jack away from opposing bowls or to 'rest out' (knock away) a bowl or bowls near the jack.

Traditionally in English bowls the third man is used to clear the head so that his skip may have adequate room to score or save with his bowls. This implies he must be better than average with his firm shots and one can scarcely disagree with this theory.

However, overseas players have shown their British brethren that the need for aggression can often be seen before eight bowls have been delivered and it is becoming customary for the number two to adopt forceful methods. This throws the onus of scoring towards the third man, so demanding accuracy in drawing to the jack.

So we are back to acceptance that the third man must be an all rounder so far as shots are concerned. He must possess good 'nerve' and a strong measure of tranquillity, to say nothing of mental stamina. Time and again one sees a third man and his skip 'carry' an out of form lead and number two for 15 ends or so, only to falter in the closing stages.

Inevitably, this shines out more in the skip than the third man but the third man can be the key factor in a close match.

So far as team selectors are concerned, I believe they should study carefully how faithfully a third man produces the shots demanded by his skip. A fine draw to the jack may earn loud applause from the bank but who can claim it was a good shot if, in actuality, the skip had called for a yard on, jack-runner. I think, maybe, that if anyone asked me the most important single technical attribute in a third man, I would answer control of length, with control of direction a minute distance behind.

So to the last man in a four, the skip, or, as he is called in Australia, the captain or rink director. Whether it be pairs, triples or fours, responsibility for overall strategy and the end by end tactics which endeavour to implement that broad conception lies with the skip.

Consequently he must be a first-class tactician but above that he must possess immense temperamental strengths: patience, tolerance, compassion, perseverance, indomitability, enthusiasm and, occasionally, an iron hand in a velvet glove.

Not to the degree of one internationally famous champion whom I once saw in the middle of an E.B.A. final at Mortlake give his out-of-form third man a public lesson in delivery. Far from helping, it crushed the self-conscious fellow so completely that what was poor form immediately deteriorated into disaster.

By all means give a rink member advice if he is committing technical mistakes; nervousness often causes a man to jerk up too soon in over anxiety to see where his bowl is going. In such cases tell the bowler—but quietly and in a suggestive rather than dogmatic manner. For, above all else, a skip must nurture everyone's confidence—and saving a man's 'face' is vital in this.

It should go without saying that the skip should possess every shot in the book—and the courage to bring them off when the chips are down. It is all very well to achieve a brilliant six or seven shot conversion with the last bowl of the match when you are leading 27–21 or some such score. But what about when it is 20 all and your club is, on aggregate, one shot behind over the other five rinks? That is the moment which sorts the men from the boys.

A really alert skip should know the physical characteristics of the actual bowls used by the members of his four. Then he will be aware, say, that his lead's bowls are straight, those of his number two possess an average draw and his third man's a wide sweep. Then he will be able not merely to indicate a general line but to stand in a position that indicates the precise line along which delivery should be made. In indicating, incidentally, a skip should give his man ample time to see.

In reality, this may be a little far fetched for actual play but the principle is correct and a skilled skip should be of immense help to any rink member who is struggling for direction.

There is no limit to the tactical-positional situations which can arise. Specifically, a good tactician seeks to impose his greatest strengths against his opponent's severest weaknesses. In fours play there are potential strengths and weaknesses in each of four opponents.

One example should suffice to reveal the general attitude to be recommended. The opposing lead may be more accurate in drawing to short jacks than your own lead but in all other positions you may hold the whip hand. So your decision must rest on whether it is preferable to give the opposing four quick ascendancy on each end and hope to outbowl them subsequently or if you should instruct your lead to switch to long jacks.

There are 16 bowls per end in fours. As a skip you should think in sixteens rather than fours or eights.

A skip must always be aware of those dangerous lies in which one good shot by the opponent can change a favourable head into one which costs a lot of shots.

Then, being aware of them, he must know when to gamble on the opponent trying, failing and suffering a drop in morale as against playing safe with protective bowls.

The finest example of that approach I've ever seen came not in fours but in singles when David Bryant beat John Scadgell in the final of the 1965 E.I.B.A. singles championship at Croydon.

Bryant drew three shots but Scadgell had an obvious jack trailer for a conversion. A careful, unthinking bowler would probably have put a bowl behind the jack for safety. Instead, Bryant drew a fourth shot and left the jack trailer on, reasoning that if Scadgell succeeded a calculated risk would have failed. On the other hand, if Scadgell failed he, Scadgell, would suffer psychologically.

The ploy succeeded beyond Bryant's wildest expectations for Scadgell caught the jack right on the nose, only for it to cannon off one of the waiting back woods and then run backwards to Bryant's four for a maximum score and disastrous effect on poor Scadgell's morale.

Lucky? Of course, but in games fortune so often favours the brave and adventurous competitor.

Additionally, a bold approach to play unquestionably breeds confidence while a careful attitude eventually lessens the performance of all but the most strong-minded of players.

All this infers that the best skips are 80 per cent students of human nature and 20 per cent actual players, though that 20 per cent must be good.

Last, but by no means least, a skip must be completely sincere. One quiet sentence, spoken with compassion and understanding, will do more for a team mate's morale than the finest psychological lecture delivered without any feeling.

And that, surely, is what skipping is all about.

6

The Seven Shots

There are seven shots used in bowls, namely the draw, trail, rest, wick, cannon, firing shot (drive), and block.

They can, with some degree of truth, be divided into two categories, one comprising those delivered with insufficient strength to reach the ditch, the other those delivering a bowl which will run into the ditch if unimpeded.

The draw, as the name implies, is one in which the deliverer's bowl has just the right weight and direction to curve its way down the green before drawing in against the jack. If it actually touches the jack it should be marked with chalk to show it is a 'toucher' and, therefore, still live if driven into the ditch.

There is only one way to become proficient at drawing to the jack and that is by scientific, purposeful practice using systems advocated earlier in this book.

However, in assessing the goodness of a draw account must be taken of the speed of the green. If it is so fast that, over a 30 yards start to stop, a bowl will trickle for 20 seconds, any bowl finishing within 3 feet of the jack must be considered good.

On the other hand, if a bowl starts and stops over 30 yards in 10 seconds, a bowl 3 inches from the jack is by no means exceptional.

However, a long running (fast) green takes a great deal of bias while a heavy, slow running green allows little or no time for the bias to work and a bowl smack in front of the jack is very difficult to beat with another draw.

Fast greens—in Britain those of 14 or more seconds—are responsive to fine gradations of touch and so they allow a skilled, sensitive bowler to exploit his finesse.

I have also explained earlier why bowls made of lignum vitae run longer, power for power, than those moulded from plastic compositions.

Indoor greens are normally faster than outdoor grass greens. Therefore, if you are a serious, scientific, ambitious bowler, you cannot better a development schedule that includes many sessions of indoor practice with lignum bowls. That indeed should heighten your sensitivity of touch but beware of playing indoor competitive matches with lignums because they are easily displaced on a fast surface and this can easily result in a damaging loss of confidence.

Never overlook the value of mental rehearsal so, whether in practice, or match play, always while standing on the mat imagine your bowl going down the green and curving in on the jack—even will it to do so. Then, and only then, repeat the imaginary delivery in actuality. Such imagining sends electric currents through the nerves in precisely the same way as the actual physical movement. Thus mental rehearsal has a definite physiological effect as well as a psychological one.

A word of warning, however. It does demand intense concentration, perhaps even greater concentration than in actually delivering the bowl itself.

Many men are, effectively, one length only bowlers. Give them that length jack and they put bowl after bowl right by it. Vary the length by a few feet and they are hopelessly at sea. Yet drawing to the jack should embrace all lengths. Consistent accuracy depends on bowling with the right amount of strength time after time. To do this one requires a personal yardstick and some bowlers endeavour to acquire this through arm swing alone. David Bryant has a better system because the length of his back swing is directly related to the length of the step he intends taking and this step, in its turn, is governed by the length of the jack and the pace of the green.

Thus on a 16 seconds green with a 25 yards jack, his step—shuffle is a better word—forward with the left leg is very short while his delivery arm travels only a few inches back past his right leg. Thus his power is always directly related to the length of his step which, in turn, governs his swing. So he is always bowling with the backing of an established yardstick.

Variations of length can be attained through use of the middle finger, for this possesses considerable strength. How effective this method can be depends to some degree on the grip used—and here I want to avoid the use of terms like cradle and claw because they are insufficiently explicit.

Just as golfers or tennis players 'feel' the shafts of their clubs or the handles of their rackets—and thus the impact of the ball—in minutely varying parts of their fingers and hands, so do bowlers experience touch in differing manners. Thus with some 'feel' is right in the finger-tips while with others it may be the fleshy part of the palm or even the heel of the hand up near the wrist. There are dozens of other sensitive spots scattered around this area.

Furthermore, there are bowlers who have a pendulum or machine-like conception of delivery which takes little or no account of a human factor like touch. They seek control of length by control of the entire pendulum.

This, I believe, demands tremendous control of leg movement and balance. Many bowlers suffered soccer or rugger leg injuries or maybe those creaks and crackles in the knee are simply caused through increasing age. Yet only if a bowler using the upright delivery is completely free of joint and muscle restrictions and is sufficiently supple of body to get down smoothly when delivering can he expect to maintain accuracy throughout one end, let alone an entire match.

Better, perhaps, to change to a semi-crouch delivery for drawing to the jack, for it is as essential for a bowler to deliver off a solid foundation as it is for an 88 mm. gun when firing at an intruder flying at supersonic speed.

These paragraphs are not intended to recommend this, that or the other method of grip or delivery but merely to set out all the factors involved. The individual—if he is ambitious—must make his choice after relating his personal attitudes to the foregoing.

Broadly speaking, a man who has good finger touch may beneficially employ finger control for variations of length while a pendulum type delivery will possibly find other methods superior.

Because this book is concerned with high achievement, it is possibly apposite to outline a few thoughts concerning the psychological relationships between a man and the delivery he uses.

This is a profound subject which I have studied in depth for tennis but not yet for bowls.

To set you thinking, men may be classified into many different categories, broad or scientifically subtle. In this instance broad concepts must suffice.

For example, some men are sensitive rather than coldly scientific. I would place John Scadgell in this category. As such he is unlikely to be a successful exponent of a mathematically precise method of delivery. He is an inspired bowler and, therefore, has an instinctive delivery style compared with, say, Tom Fleming whose great successes in the Vitalite, World Drawing to the Jack Tournament was founded on machine-like precision.

Let me emphasize that this is an over-simplification. It is intended merely to make you think about the relationship of your personality as a man to your way of playing bowls. It can have quite a significant effect in situations which demand fine differences of technique—and nothing demands these more than consistent length control.

It is fair to say that the draw shot is normally less spectacular than the rest-out or the jack trailer.

In both the last two cases you are bowling to move a specific target, viz. an opponent's bowl or the jack. Consequently, the delivery has to be fractionally stronger than a dead draw.

Since the bowl will still be travelling when it hits its target, the bias will not yet have brought about maximum curvature of your bowl. Thus the approach line will differ slightly.

The amount of that variation is dependent on two factors, the distance you wish to move the target and the pace of the green.

For instance, if the green is a slow, 10 seconds, and you only wish to run the jack 3 inches, you might just as well consider your shot a draw just through the jack and, therefore, not worry about change of line. On the other hand, if it is a 16-seconds green and you plan to move an opposing bowl 4 feet, the necessary weight will cause a change of delivery line wider than the diameter of the jack. So a little mental computing will be called for.

In general, rest-out shots are usually made with a wish for the delivered bowl to stay in position after knocking the target bowl away. So the delivered bowl should have slight underspin imparted during delivery and this is scarcely possible without use of the thumb to grip the bowl. Thus a cradle grip is less suited to this than a claw.

Using the thumb enables you to slide your fingers under the bowl slightly at the moment of release down on the green—no bumping, please, and be sure that back knee is also well down and the front upper leg parallel with the ground—so imparting early skid.

This skid alters the time ratio between the first and second halves of the bowl's travel and so, in effect, reduces its follow through after impact.

In jack trailing you normally want the bowl to run with the jack. This is helped by top spin which, in turn, is helped better by a cradle grip than by the claw; the bowl rolls out of the hand instead of skidding out.

Nevertheless, the majority of such shots are essentially over strength draw shots corrected in direction for the changed curvature of the run relative to the length of the jack.

Fundamentally, the wick and cannon are variations of the rest since all have a bowl as their target. However, while in resting out you endeavour either to drop on to the target, so replacing it as the bowl nearer to the jack or pushing it out of position and staying put yourself, the wick and cannon are more concerned with where the delivered bowl finishes after contacting the target bowl.

Really, both are the same, the wick merely representing contact with a smaller section of the target bowl—say an eighth or

G   97

sixteenth of its diameter—while the cannon approximates to a half ball in-off at billiards.

At billiards, however, it is possible over the relatively small length of the table to impart via the cue such severe underspin (screw) that your ball returns straight back along the line it took to the target ball.

Such underspin or skid is scarcely possible over, say, 30 yards with a bowl delivered by hand.

So the majority of wicks and cannons come off the target bowl at standard angles governed by the weight, size and basic material of the two bowls.

Thus a bowl hitting a minimum diameter, maximum weight, slightly elliptical Henselite will come off at a wider angle than if hitting a lignum bowl of similar diameter but lighter weight.

Maybe this sounds too academic and scientific to be of practical value on a bowling green where it is seldom possible to deliver with precision equalling that seen in billiards.

Remember, though, this book is concerned with winning, with becoming a champion. Champions in all the games with which I have been concerned differ from those below them in a number of ways, one of which is in an infinite capacity for taking pains. That capacity means attention to many tiny details, many of which may result in only two or three points a year in an entire season.

But who among us cannot recall matches each season in which better ability to play a particular shot—a cannon maybe—would have changed victory into defeat.

I recall vividly David Bryant facing a match lie against Snowy Walker at Kyeemagh in the 1966 World Championships. Bryant has studied cannons with all the fervour of a billiards-snooker enthusiast and, therefore, is fully aware of how weight and spin affect angles. So he was able to deliver a fairly fast bowl which removed first one and then the other of Walker's before remaining in position for victory. It was a shot in a million and fully intended. Maybe without study and practice he would still have achieved it but I assess his chances would have been a thousand times less. So knowledge and skill acquired through attention to detail enabled him to turn defeat into victory in a match where his personal pride was as much at stake as a world title.

Observation of match play and experimental practice of cannons and wicks on the green will help you to blend these basic theories with the practicalities of play. There is no short cut, intelligent practice makes perfect.

Normally cannons are attempted with less subtleties of touch than straightforward draws to the jack. So variation of thumb position in order to improve control of direction is by no means disadvantageous.

In the firing shot direction is all important and power essential. So most champions move the thumb nearer to the top of the bowl than for any other shot.

To help power it is advantageous to adopt the upright, athletic delivery with the body flowing smoothly forward with the swing of the arm. The bowl should be cupped more deeply in the hand for, remember, it is pace you seek, not finger-tip control.

Many people have a tendency to tension in the shoulder joint and under arm when delivering. Be aware of this and consciously relax. Let the arm and body flow as smoothly as is humanly possible. Let that pendulum flow and the arm swing freely along the line to the target.

What should the target be? Here is a paradox. In drawing to the jack, the faster the green, the more the bowl curves in its run.

In firing the reverse happens. Think for a moment. Bias works when the bowl is slowing down. On a fast green a firing shot slows very little, on a slow green it decelerates appreciably. Thus bias has more effect and the bowl swerves. How much you must find out by experimenting. But, as a guide, when firing on a 14-seconds green your target is likely to be the outside edge of the target bowl—i.e. right hand side if firing on the forehand, left hand side if firing on the backhand.

Which hand to use? The choice is yours but, on the whole, the forehand is probably preferable because it is, to most bowlers, more natural than the backhand. Your natural hand is likely to be more powerful than the other hand, power is vital in firing—

and imparted by swinging, not forcing. Yes, the forehand seems the better choice.

Your delivery when drawing to the jack may be one in which your left hand rests on your left upper leg. This restricts body pivot from right to left and so reduces power. So long as accuracy is not too seriously reduced, try letting your left arm swing free when firing—at least as an experiment. However, accuracy is the ultimate need and this must never be overlooked during your efforts to develop more power.

Finally, the block, a shot little used nowadays. As its name implies, this is a bowl delivered with the aim of blocking the path to a critical bowl or part of the head.

There is always an optimum length and line for such a shot. Too short and your bowl can be swerved round. Too long and it can be cannoned forward to act in lieu of the delivered bowl.

Norman King advocates delivering such bowls on the opposite hand to the one likely to be used. Thus the bowl's final slow down will be across the line you expect the opponent to take.

On the whole, blocks are not a good 'percentage play' against draw shots because your opponent can obtain significant changes of run simply by bowling from different positions on the mat.

They are more useful in situations where your opponent is liable to fire. Firing shots travel virtually in straight lines so that a block dead on course can completely ruin the effects of firing shots.

Nevertheless, the demands on accuracy are so great that I believe blocks to be of greater use psychologically than actually. They 'get in the eye' of your opponent and, bearing this in mind, will appear bigger when in isolation half-way up the green than when nearer to the head.

A final beware. Do not use a block shot which forces your opponent to use his best and strongest shot when a normally placed bowl will tempt him to use a weaker shot—maybe a draw instead of a drive. . . . But that is more a question of tactics than technique.

7

The Different Games

Bowls championships staged under International Bowling Board laws use four events, singles, pairs, triples, and fours. Of these the man-to-man clash of singles is the strongest crowd puller. And with each man sending down four bowls, it is the game which provides more spectacular shots than the others.

True, in pairs—two players in each team—each man delivers four bowls, but that results in heads of sixteen bowls. These leave far less room for subtle shots than when there are only eight clustered near the jack. Indeed, there can only be seven before the last bowl is sent down the green towards the head in a singles match.

Four shots per end give more chance of finding correct land and length and a less crowded head offers better chances of finding a path to targets. Thus the more dramatic clash of man versus man is supplemented, on average, by better bowling so that the appeal of singles to a spectator is doubly strong compared with the other three games.

Additionally, each bowler is responsible for 50 per cent of the bowls per end and is engaged 50 per cent of the playing time. This compares with four bowls out of sixteen in pairs and 25 per cent of playing time, three bowls out of eighteen in triples and $16\frac{2}{3}$ per cent of the playing time and two bowls out of sixteen in fours or $12\frac{1}{2}$ per cent of playing time.

Generally speaking, this deeper involvement assists both play and concentration, another reason why singles matches produce a greater number of spectacular shots, generally speaking.

This, of course, works in a negative way also. Thus many fine four-wood bowlers are far less effective in fours when they only deliver two bowls per end.

This leads naturally to the idea that many bowlers waste their first two bowls in singles and I was specially gratified by a paragraph written once by that great bowler John Scadgell. I noticed once when he was going through one of those rough spells that stars in all games occasionally suffer that over anxiety was causing him to hurry his first two bowls each end. I suggested this to him quietly and two or three years later he entered on a research questionnaire that this was the best piece of bowls advice he had ever been given.

If a gold winning Commonwealth Games bowler of immense experience can fall into this trap, how much likelier is this to happen to an ambitious bowler on the way up?

This, I fancy, leads to a maxim which applies to all games including bowls. It derives from the old saw, 'Tall oaks from little acorns grow.' Translated into bowls parlance, it means great wins are achieved through successions of good shots so treat every single bowl you deliver as one of tremendous importance.

In singles especially, men who produce one real dazzler and three stinkers per end sometimes beat opponents who inexorably put down four good bowls per end. But if you watch the E.B.A. Championships year after year you will discover that consistent accuracy usually leads to the President's congratulations and the winner's trophy.

That is why David Bryant has such a phenomenal record. Of course he delivers bad bowls. Naturally he makes errors of judgement. But he never delivers a careless, thoughtless bowl. And because each delivery springs from the utmost care and concentration, 90 per cent of them are effective. For him, forgetting the mistake just made and the next bowl to come while concentrating fully on the one actually in his hand has built up, bowl by bowl, end by end, match by match, a record that may never be beaten.

Triples play entails special problems because there are eighteen bowls per end instead of the sixteen in pairs and fours. So the congestion around the jack is considerable.

Because of this, perhaps the follow through shot is the one of greatest use. As in billiards, the object is for your bowl to strike a target bowl, push it out of the way but, instead of replacing it, to run through to a scoring or favourable lie.

This is true also in pairs and fours play but in the latter, with only two bowls to deliver, one is perhaps a little chary of being too ambitious. Yet such shots demand complete, full-hearted confidence if they are to stand the best chance of success.

Until recently, it has been customary to regard bowls as a type of mobile chess with all kinds of positional plays as a natural part of this conception. But Scotland's successes in the annual International Team Championship and those of fours from Hong Kong, Australia and New Zealand in individual championships suggests that positive attacks on the jack are possibly more effective. Not that I am in any way suggesting a boycott of positional play but I do sometimes get a strong impression that players are so obsessed with position that they relegate in importance or even forget altogether that the object of the game is to deliver as many bowls as possible nearer to the jack than the best of the opponents'.

By all means protect undefended back positions. If you are well ahead, consider pairing each of your bowls with each of the opponents. But do keep the game simple. Complicating it so often results in failure to attain objectives.

However, tactics are so dependent on situations and circumstances that practical experiences, perhaps, provide the best lessons. So in the next chapter I am reprinting some of the articles which appeared in *World Bowls* magazine under the title 'My Greatest End'.

8

Their Greatest Ends

Bill Gillis, the English International, tells his story

The end I recall more than any other, the one that gave me my greatest thrill, was during the international match against Ireland in 1956, the year I captained England. I was up against an Irish rink that had Tom Henry as No. 3, with Syd Thompson skip.

England held a very commanding lead in the overall game.

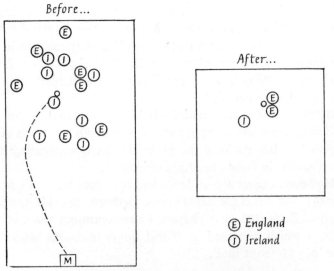

Fig. 13. This is the end that England international Bill Gillis describes.

Then Ireland began a magnificent recovery and were gradually on our heels, only a few shots separating the teams and every shot vital.

At our nineteenth end the position was as in my diagram. Thompson drew the winner with his last wood. England had laid two shots until this occurred. His wood, a toucher, looked as if it would fall any time but didn't.

I was left with a very delicate situation. I felt like throwing my last wood away giving the shot to Ireland as the least over weight on to the winner would result in the jack gliding off our wood to three Irish woods just beyond our two previous winners.

After a quick look at the scoreboards I realized I must try and play a perfect length wood to just make the Irish one fall.

I thought I was going to fail, but my wood just reached the winner, making it fall and it pushed the jack to our previous two winners leaving England a very welcome 2—and there was a very sporting cheer from the Irish supporters for the greatest wood I ever bowled.

Percy Baker, four times E.B.A. Singles Champion

My greatest end? There have been so many that I find it most difficult to decide which was the greatest.

There were some terrific shots played in the last few ends of the 1952 National Singles final against Algy Allen. But I think perhaps the 1946 final will always remain in my memory.

The game was 19–16 in my favour and I lay two shots and game, Ernie Newton had last wood, and he took out one, leaving the score 20–16.

Ernie favoured a full length and scored two singles, making it 20–18. On the next end he lay shot and, in trying a run-through shot on a short bowl, I pushed him in another, making it 20-all. Another full-length jack.

Newton played the forehand N1 and N2 (see Fig. 14) arc both scoring. B1 and B2 played on backhand arc in a very good position, but do not count.

N3 was intended to block the backhand draw but ran across, still leaving just enough room to get through.

I now had to decide (with my third wood) the backhand draw with every chance of being wrecked or a follow through on N1 or 2.

Had it been my last wood, I would certainly have gone for the follow through but having already played twice on backhand, my first wood running only a few inches out of count, now there was an opening between N2 and N3 and the invitation to draw between them was too strong to resist.

I played it, and you will see from my diagram, it was a peach. It ran between N2 and 3 as intended, pushed the jack some 2 or 3 inches back to bring B1 in as second wood.

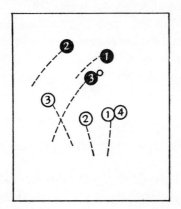

Fig. 14. Baker's bowls shaded; Newton's unshaded.

I well remembering hearing Ernie say to his supporters, on returning from inspecting the head, 'he's got me this time'.

It seems the only hope left to Newton was a dead draw. There was just about room to get round N1 but only with a dead length. This he tried, but was short, N4.

I had last wood but fortunately no need to use it.

Harold Burbage, England Indoor International
The occasion was the pairs semi-final of the Tithe Barn open tournament in 1960. My partner was Eddie Woollven, of Little-

hampton, and our opponents were the well-known Sussex bowlers, Cecil and Henry Salisbury.

During the day we had already played three rounds, and the tournament organizers wanted this semi-final completed, to facilitate final arrangements for the next day as I was doing well in the singles.

At 8.45 it was getting dusk, the score stood at 20-all and we were playing the last end.

I had one wood left, with the opposing skip to follow me. I could either fire and try to break the end, or I could try to draw wide round the front woods and on the opponents' shot wood with sufficient strength to move the jack a maximum distance of 5 inches. Any distance more than 5 inches would give the opponents two shots. (See Fig. 15.)

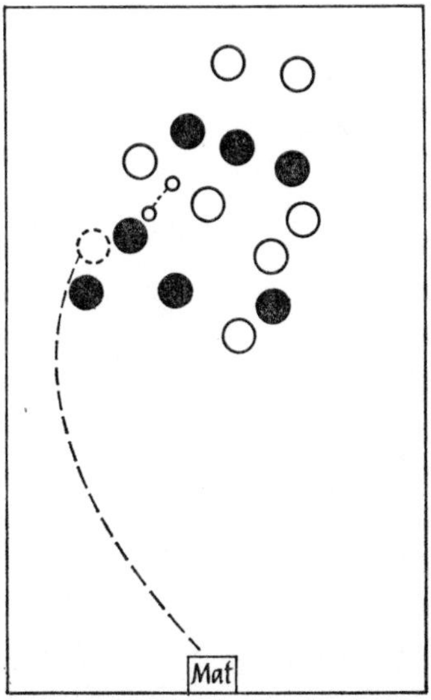

Fig. 15. Burbage's woods are those unshaded.

Having viewed the head and spoken to Woollven it was decided I should endeavour to play the draw.

The light was by now getting bad but I did have the satisfaction of seeing my wood curl round the front woods and the result was the jack moved 4 inches.

107

This shot gave us two making the score 22–20. I then had to wait while the opposing skip delivered his last wood. He was unsuccessful with a firm wood to break the end.

This end was played in a full-length jack and considering the conditions, time and tiredness, etc., the shot gave me great joy, for, afterwards, we went on to win the final.

Bob Cowan, Scottish International

My greatest end was probably one in the pairs at the 1948 Hastings tournament.

My partner, H. Black, and I got to the finals when we met Croal and Birtles and had a great game.

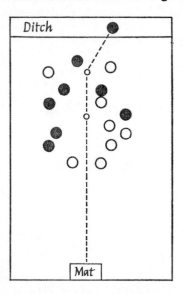

Fig. 16. The end Bow Cowan describes—his bowls are those shaded.

After the twenty-first end, we were all-square and an extra end had to be played.

My partner, Black, and Birtles were leading and drawing to the jack in splendid fashion, and while the opposition were holding two shots, Croal told Birtles to try to cover the jack with a short bowl.

This, he just failed to do by finishing about 4 feet short and a

108

little narrow. I had played a bowl through the head, about 2 yards, while Croal put in another short bowl a little wide leaving a space of about 12 inches between his and Birtles'.

With my last bowl I had no alternative but drive up through that port, got the jack right through, caught the through bowl I had played, and the jack bounced up in the air about 4 feet and dropped close to the same bowl for game.

All that Croal could say was 'the luck of the bounce off the jack against the bowl and remaining there'.

Arthur Philby, winner of the 1963 British Isles Pairs Championship (with Charlie Plater)

Having been playing bowls since 1922, it is almost impossible to remember what was 'my greatest end', but certainly the one I now describe is the one that gave me the greatest thrill.

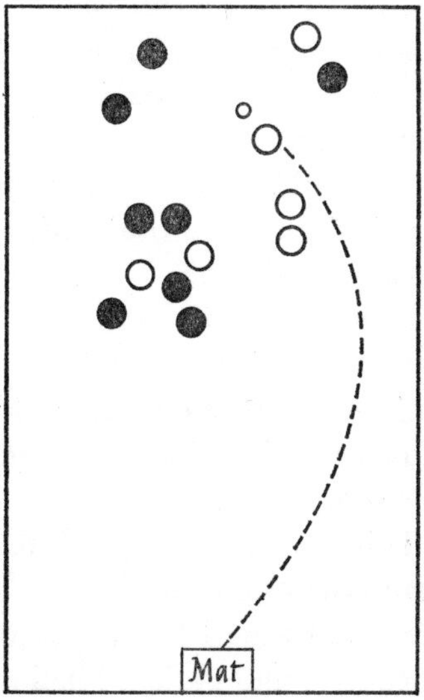

Fig. 17. The end Arthur Philby describes, the dotted line showing his side winning draw.

It was in the 1960 National Pairs Championship at Mortlake when Charlie Plater and I defeated S. Morley and Ken Cooper of Notts in the quarter-finals.

109

At the twentieth end, the game stood 17–17. Charlie put his first wood of the twenty-first end 1 foot short of the jack—which was a full-length one—at about 5 o'clock. He also put another one almost touching this.

These woods did not lie right for promotion because, if they were touched, they would have gone across the face of the jack and not up to it.

Charlie's first wood laid shot until the fourth wood from Morley promoted another one of his own to about 6 inches from the jack at 1 o'clock. This laid shot until my last wood.

With my first wood I tried to draw round Charlie's two short woods on to the shot wood 6 inches beyond the jack but without much hope of success as I felt I should be wrecked.

Having failed with this first wood, I decided to scatter Charlie's two woods to have an open draw. I had two woods at this and just failed to make contact.

I was, therefore, left with the same position with which I had started the end. I would point out that when we played the forehand in this direction we all took about 1 yard of green but, as I was walking back to the mat, I recalled that I had played a wood, during the trial end, twice this width and it had come back beautifully.

I, therefore, thought that if I could get the same green with my last wood it would, in all probability, pass Charlie's woods and, with correct weight, curl in for shot.

This it did, and we won a most interesting game by the aid of this shot 18–17.

This gave me a great deal of pleasure, because it meant we were now sure of an E.B.A. Championship prize. This was the thirteenth time I had appeared in the National Championship since 1946 and though I had reached two quarter-finals this was the first time I had qualified for a prize.

Who said thirteen is unlucky?

Another thrill for me was that Charlie stepped across the head and shook hands with me. This was the only time in the thirteen

110

years I played with him that, win or lose, he had ever shown anything but an ice-cold temperament.

Bill Hart, Captain of England in 1961

The end that I recall was in many ways a dramatic one. I was playing in the Essex County Association triples final in 1958, and it was Southend versus Essex County Club on the Ilford green.

Southend's team was F. Lear, H. Owen, W. E. Hart. Essex County Club team: P. Smith, G. Bridgstock, E. Clay.

Though Southend as a club had won every other honour in Essex they had never won the triples championship.

It was a very sultry afternoon, and we were playing on the No. 6 rink, which had a very big draw on the one side. We had

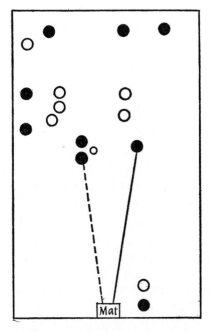

Fig. 18. Dotted line shows both woods taken away with Hart's second; unbroken line shows one taken away by last wood.

111

played seventeen ends, and the score was Southend 10, Essex County Club 15.

Then, after fourteen woods had been played, Bridgstock for some unknown reason asked Clay for another back wood instead of trying to get among our five woods that were lying behind the jack at a distance of 2 feet to $1\frac{1}{2}$ yards.

With my second wood, having failed with the first, I succeeded in getting their two woods both away from the jack without disturbing the jack with a drive. Clay drew second wood just about 2 feet at the right of the jack with his last wood.

I had the choice of trailing the jack for six or taking his wood away to lay five. I chose the latter, and succeeded making five shots to bring the score 15–15 with an extra end to be played.

Owen drew a perfect shot with his second which we, with our remaining woods, successfully covered up for Southend to win the triples championship for the first time, 16–15.

This in no way could be a great end, but definitely one where the chance had to be taken. There were a lot of spectators at this Essex final, and many have reminded me of this end.

Leslie Watson, former member of the English team for the Empire Games

My greatest end? This is not an easy question to answer, but I shall always remember very vividly the end that was certainly the most thrilling and vital I have experienced.

The place—the Paddington Bowling Club. The occasion—the final of the E.B.A. National Pairs Championship. The time—about 6 p.m. on Wednesday, 22nd August 1956.

My brother Harry and I were playing against the late Ernie Pullin, the Wiltshire international, and his son Alec. The game had been very close all through and was again level after the nineteenth end. We scored a single at the twentieth and thus came to the last end one shot in front.

The position when Ernie went to play his last wood was shot and game in our favour and so—as he had done twice previously —he fired and cannoned the jack for a dead end.

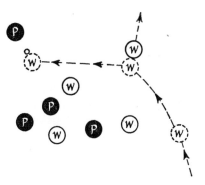

Fig. 19. This is the end Leslie Watson describes.

The end was replayed and this time, when Pullin and I had one wood each to play, the situation of the woods in front of and in the near proximity of the jack was as shown in my diagram, with the shot laid against us, about 2 inches behind the jack to make the scores level.

We were second shot, but Ernie Pullin had last wood and a reasonable chance to draw another shot for game and the championship.

The route was barred for a draw to beat the shot wood, there was grave risk of promoting one of our opponents' short woods if I attempted a follow through. And, similarly, to drive was not the answer as the match could so easily be given away if I took out our second shot or promoted one of theirs.

There seemed to be only one chance of beating the shot wood. We had a wood about 2 feet short of the jack on the forehand, at 4 o'clock. A half ball in-off was on and I decided to try it.

As soon as the wood left my hand I sensed it had possibilities and followed it up hopefully. To the delight of my brother and myself, my wood connected with the target wood at just the right angle, cannoned very gently to the left, and rolled slowly on to finish sitting right on the jack, but without disturbing it.

Ernie Pullin fired to try and make another dead end. But, this time, he missed narrowly and we had won the title.

Walter Phillips, captain of England in the 1962 international series at Glasgow

My greatest end? . . . This is not a very easy question to answer, but after considerable thought I have chosen this one as having a great bearing on the result of a game.

The last time I was able to play in that grand June tournament held at Weston-super-Mare, I had a particularly thrilling game with Tommy Hims, from Worcester. This happened on the Friday afternoon in the quarter-finals. News around the greens had come to me that he was playing very good bowls and had knocked several top-class bowlers out, so I was quite prepared for what was to come.

The crowd must have sensed that a battle was taking place for the banks became crowded to overflowing. The rink allotted to us was an end one, but the draw on both sides was excellent.

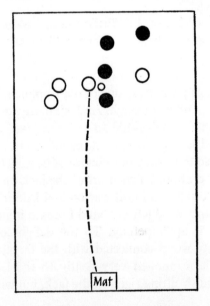

Fig. 20. This is the end Walter Phillips describes. His bowls are shown in white with Hims' in black.

We kept very close to one another until the score read 19–18 in my favour. I am sure that many of the spectators there that afternoon will remember the following end.

Having won the previous one, it was my turn to deliver the first bowl to a nearly full-length jack, this finished about 9 inches away from the jack (jack high). Tommy's first finished 2 feet behind the jack.

My second bowl finished near my first and things were looking good for me. But now it was Tommy who took a hand in affairs and his second bowl came to rest about 5 inches past the jack for shot.

My third went a trifle narrow and missed the head altogether. My opponent then pulled a great shot out of the bag, drew on to the jack pressing it back to his other bowl, each being only a $\frac{1}{4}$ inch from the kitty, one in front, one behind—no target.

This made him lying two shots, making him, at the moment, 20 and one bowl from each to come.

This left me only a single bowl at which to aim if I attempted to fire with no position at the rear. So, after careful inspection, I decided to draw with the hope that if I was a trifle wide I might slide in to the jack off my two jack high woods.

This did not happen as I found the exact green and drew dead to the jack, my bowl gently falling in on to my opponent's bowls which kept it propped up and touching the jack for shot. Tommy's last bowl missed the target only by inches and was 20.

The necessary one shot came at the next end—for which I was really thankful.

Tom Brown, England World Championship team, 1966

In the past, I have taken part in many notable games, but I have to go back to 1951 for my most thrilling end. Even after all this time, the details remain fresh in my memory.

Wally Bates and I, of Woking Park, were playing a strong pair from Weybridge Rec., Darkie Goree and his partner, in the Surrey pairs. They were a stronger combination than Wally and

I and always had us on the defensive. Playing the eighteenth end, we had done very well to hold them to a seven-shot lead.

With my last wood to be played at this end, we were lying one shot, 4 inches from the jack, with our opponents lying three very close seconds.

They were obviously content to hold us to one shot, confident that a six-shot lead over the last three ends would see them safely through.

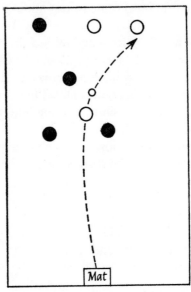

Fig. 21. This is the end Tom Brown describes. He and his partner's woods are shown white, their opponents' black.

I rather shared this opinion and suggested to Wally that I should attempt to force the shot wood through with the jack towards two back woods of ours.

Wally was rather horrified at the risks involved and pointed out that any mistake was practically fatal to our chances. But in the end, he reluctantly agreed.

The result exceeded even my wildest expectations, the forcing wood following through to make four shots.

We were inspired by this sudden success, our opponents were dazed by it and we went on to win by two shots.

Douglas Adamson, former Scottish international

Though the shot I am about to describe was not the best I have ever made it was probably the most vital. It was played during the final for the Gibson-Watt trophy at the Llandrindod Wells tournament in August 1960. My opponent was the well-known English international, A. W. Knowling, of Worthing.

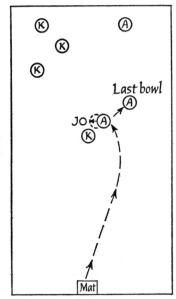

Fig. 22. Douglas Adamson's bowls are marked 'A' and Knowling's shown 'K'.

During the game I was going through a sticky patch and was trailing 11–13. With Arthur's wood lying 2 inches from the jack, my own wood was 6 inches from it, slightly beyond, jack high.

With the position of the head I could not play a yard-on shot as I could take away my own wood and lose four.

I decided to play to raise my own wood half a turn towards

the jack. I tried with my third wood and just slipped past. With my last, I raised my wood the exact half turn and gained one shot.

The danger was that I could have lost a three or four by running my opponent's wood and the jack into his back woods.

Fortunately, this particular shot gave me the necessary confidence to go on and record a victory.

Paddy Orr, 1953 and 1955 Surrey singles champion

I am not very keen on post-mortems on matches, whether successful or otherwise, but I vividly recall two ends in the Surrey singles final at Balham in 1953.

My opponent was Ken Coulson, already established as one of Surrey's best bowlers. Ken had skipped the Surrey fours champions at Balham the previous year and in 1951 had contested the county singles final with Jack Killick. I had been knocking at the door in Surrey competitions and had first been badged in 1953 following my success in the 1952 Surrey unbadged singles. Selection as a No. 2 in the 1953 Surrey Middleton Cup side had given me that necessary extra confidence for this singles battle with Ken.

In the early stages we were both jockeying for position and getting the feel of the green, but with the score 6–4 in Ken's favour he held three shots and I had one wood to play.

The forehand was open but I gambled on a delicate trailing shot over to my two woods which had finished wide and a couple of feet through on the forehand. (See diagram 23.) It came off and I had a slender lead instead of being 4–9 down. Seizing the initiative on three-quarter length jacks I increased my advantage to 18–12.

Ken fought back and, after scoring, switched to short jacks. His greater experience on these brought him dangerously near with the score 19–18 in my favour.

To my surprise, he threw a three-quarter jack and I lay two shots with only one wood each left to play.

Ken, with his last wood, drew slightly narrow on the forehand

and came to rest a few inches through and about 18 inches from the jack.

That wood could bring Ken level and was robbing me of victory. Should I attempt to draw for a possible single or gamble on firing this wood out?

As I walked back to the mat I kept telling myself: 'Either draw or fire. There must be no compromise shot!'

I decided on the firing shot. The forehand was open and the more obvious hand on which to execute this shot.

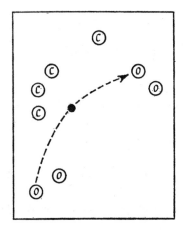

Fig. 23.   Fig. 24.

Paddy Orr's bowls are marked 'O' and Coulson's shown 'C'.

Two short woods on the backhand narrowed the angle, but the forehand had proved slightly unreliable throughout the match, so I decided on the backhand.

Two short woods on the backhand narrowed the single, but the forehand had proved slightly unreliable throughout the match, so I decided on the backhand.

Then came the crucial moment. The wood left my hand with some force—Ken swears I bumped it—struck Ken's wood on the shoulder and both woods went out of the rink in opposite directions without disturbing the head. (See Fig. 24.)

I raced after my wood and, as it sped unerringly for the target, triumphantly cried: 'I've got it!'

At the same time Luigi Manzi, the Temple Club's famous Italian member, was excitedly jumping up and down with arms aloft on the bank and shouting: 'He's got it!'

Surrey president Joe Wilson (Mid-Surrey), the marker, and Ken almost incredulously examined the shot where my thunderbolt had struck.

Unfortunately for Ken, I had removed his wood as clean as a whistle.

Perhaps it was a dramatic way to snatch victory, but I had felt instinctively that if Ken had drawn level the psychological advantage would have enabled him to go on to win.

Harold Shapland, former president of the E.B.A.

Even if I live to be 150 I do not think I will ever forget the shot I had to play at the end of Devon's third round Middleton Cup tie against Wiltshire on the Victoria Club Green at Weston-super-Mare back in 1950.

It was the last rink of the match to finish and when Ernie Pullen (Wilts) went to the mat for the last time, Devon were three up on the other rinks and holding perhaps one shot on mine.

Ernie drew perfectly on the backhand and carried the jack through to a nest of four Wiltshire woods. So Wiltshire had an overall lie of one for game.

Referring to the Devonshire County Handbook for 1951 I read: 'Imagine the breathtaking scene. Harold Shapland delivering the last wood of the match. All around the bank and adjoining greens the vast number of players, officials and supporters, standing mute, like statues, hardly daring to breathe. The whole of Wiltshire hoping that the vital wood would prove a failure, and Devon praying hard for a miracle. And there on the mat was the lone figure with the issue of the match in his hands.

'Wiltshire's skip, Pullen, had just delivered his last wood, trailing the jack to three back woods, leaving Wiltshire one shot ahead. Harold had to draw a perfect full-length shot, in between two short woods, around the main portion of the head, on to the jack—the white jade of destiny—lying safe and secure in the midst of four Wiltshire woods.'

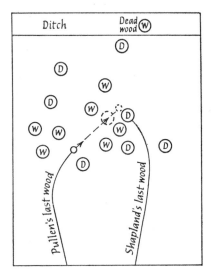

Fig. 25. The end Harold Shapland describes. Devon's woods are marked 'D'; Wiltshire's 'W'.

Those two woods out in front looked awfully close together and I could see very little of the jack. Yet even as I stood on the mat I knew there was only one shot to try, a full-length draw.

So I got the wood off on the forehand and what a long time it seemed to take. But I could see it was on its course and as it squeezed between the two front woods I felt it was going to curl round and get to the jack.

Sure enough it did, converting Wiltshire's four into one for Devon and so the county went through to the fourth round of the Middleton Cup.

I was fairly excited but, judging from the way everyone

swarmed round me, I think I must have been the calmest man around the green at that moment. It is a moment I will never forget.

Bobby Stenhouse, former English international from Northants
The shot that gave me the greatest satisfaction was played during the Middleton Cup match between Berkshire and Northamptonshire, at Broadmore, in June 1962.

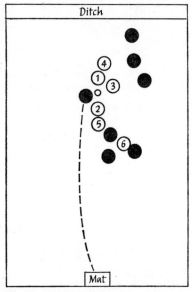

Fig. 26. Berkshire's bowls are white,
Northants' black.

My diagram shows the position of the head with the skips still to play—Berkshire lying five shots, three of which were within an inch of the jack and the jack completely hidden. The forehand was blocked and the backhand was very tricky, due to a straight run, and no one was playing it with confidence.

After consultation with my third, Alan Wintersgill, I decided to play a backhand draw in an attempt to save shots.

My first wood, played with about 6 inches of green, ran a yard through. Jack Warren, my opponent, stayed away from the head with his.

With my second I tried to play a dead length wood, knowing that the margin for error was almost nil. My wood slid past Berkshire's 5 and 2 to finish shot, jack high against the jack.

Jack played a running shot with his last wood to force my shot bowl through, but just missed. My sigh of relief was echoed by those of my colleagues.

As the game was very close at this stage, this turnover of six shots was vital for Northants.

Paddy McGuirk, Irish international

I was opposed to English skip Bill Gillis in the international at Cardiff in 1955 and one particular end in this game probably merits the title 'my greatest end'.

This is not because of great bowling in the accepted sense but rather owing to making the most of a situation that did not appear to offer very much and in which my two woods played a part.

Playing to a shortish jack and with thirteen bowls already delivered, England lay four shots. Two English woods were 3 to 5 yards short, lying in a straight line on the forehand and about a bowl's width of covering the jack.

Of our six woods played we had the four best back, lying 1 to 2 yards through also on the forehand. I was aware of the possibilities if I could take the jack through on the forehand, but from the mat the short bowls offered no margin for error.

I played the forehand with some weight and succeeded in my objective, striking the jack to within a couple of yards from the ditch, the jack finally coming to rest in the middle of the backhand, my wood running on to count first shot, and making the total in my favour five.

Gillis drew on the backhand, with his second wood finishing jack high 1 yard wide to count number one. With my remaining bowl I fired on the forehand taking the shot bowl to the ditch, my own wood going likewise, thereby regaining the five shots.

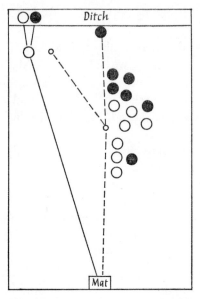

Fig. 27. In this diagram, the Irish
woods are black and England white.
Dotted rule shows McGuirk's first
wood; unbroken line, his last.

I am influenced most in quoting this end by the fact that it
involved a turnover of nine shots, an experience that one does
not meet every day particularly in the international sphere.

*Percy Watson, Northern Ireland international and past president
of the International Bowling Board*
I find it difficult to recall in detail any particular end which
could be said of itself to have produced an immediate or unexpected result, but I have still a vivid recollection of one in the
middle of a series which seemed to me to influence the ultimate
result.

It was in Vancouver in 1954 when I was, with Bill Rosbotham,
representing Northern Ireland in the Empire Games pairs.

We had won the first three matches, drawn the fourth and lost
the fifth by two shots.

We met Hong Kong in the sixth game of the series, our confidence slightly shaken by the previous day's less satisfactory results.

By the fifteenth end, an early lead had disappeared and our two worthy opponents from Hong Kong—Eric Liddell and Raul da Luz—playing with every confidence and superb skill, had gained the initiative and were dictating the game.

On the sixteenth end, when I had two bowls to play and my opponent one, Hong Kong were lying three shots. I tried what seemed to be the only worthwhile shot, one of ditch length on the backhand through a narrow port.

The result was even more fortunate than I could have hoped for, the bowl pushing the jack almost straight back to the ditch and itself coming to rest in the ditch about 4 feet away giving us a count of four shots. (See Fig. 28 (a).)

The Hong Kong skip, Raul da Luz, played a perfect forehand draw with his last bowl to get the shot about a foot from the ditch.

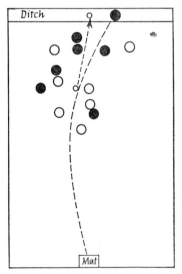
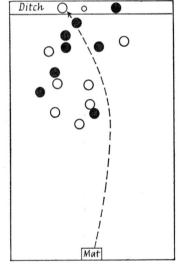

Fig. 28a.   Fig. 28b.

Northern Ireland bowls are shown black, with Hong Kong white.

With the last bowl of the end I followed on the forehand with sufficient weight to push the lying shot into the ditch and lie in its place for a final count of five. (See Fig. 28 (b).)

This substantial swing enabled us to regain the initiative and win the game. It also restored our confidence so much that we went on to win all the remaining games in the series.

I still believe that if we had failed at that end, Hong Kong would have beaten us and ended our hopes of winning that coveted gold medal.

Tom Yeoman, Welsh international

As you may already know, I won the Welsh open singles championship in 1927, 1930 and 1940. In each of these games I was opposed by a fellow Welsh international and came from behind to win on the post.

In the 1930 final, my opponent was Reg Baker. The only time I took the lead was when I reached 21.

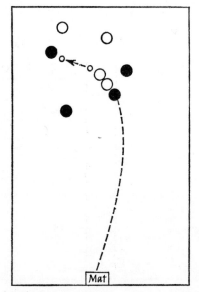

Fig. 29. Tom Yeoman's bowls are black, Baker's white.

I had trailed all through the game and the score had been called 19–13 against me. I crept up to 19–18 when I brought off my greatest shot to complete the greatest end of my long career.

The diagram illustrates the end, my bowls being black and Baker's white.

My opponent was two shots for game and his four bowls excellently placed when I had my last bowl to play. I could not force it on the forehand or backhand with any hope of getting shot.

However, I decided to play a forehand shot with sufficient strength on to my opponent's second shot to spring the jack about 18 inches.

This I did perfectly and made the score 19–19.

I finished the game by scoring two shots on the next end and so concluded my second successful Welsh open singles championship.

Algie Allen, English international

What was the greatest shot I ever played? It was probably the one that came while representing Oxford City and County in the final of the London & Southern Counties B.A., at Magdalen Park B.C. green in July 1939 against Sutton B.C., the Surrey champions (T. Stoker, S. H. Pratt and L. S. Walton).

After the thirteenth end we were trailing 14–4. Sutton were playing very well, everything coming off.

But after the fourteenth end the score stood at 14–11. My diagram shows how one bowl can make such a difference to the score.

My colleagues, the late Dr. J. Burrows and J. Holden, had failed to give me shot, but four of their bowls were lying about 18 inches behind the jack. Our opponents were lying shot, jack high, about 14 inches to the left of the jack.

I had to decide whether I would force the shot bowl through or try to draw the jack through to my colleagues' bowls.

Before my last bowl, I had a discussion with my No. 2,

Holden, and during this discussion someone among the spectators shouted: 'Go on Algie you can do it.'

I was delighted. It was the voice of John Paterson, of Surrey, who has since died. He was my skip for England.

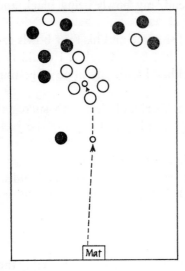

Fig. 30. The end Algie Allen describes. His club's bowls are white, his opponents' are black.

I went back to the mat full of confidence, picked up my bowl, delivered it and, to my colleagues' and my delight, trailed the jack to six of my bowls, making a score of seven.

I think this was one of my greatest shots and had the desired effect. Our opponents went to pieces, and we went on to win by seven shots, 25–18.

Vic Oliver, English international

We were suffering on our rink, struggling along at the fifteenth end being 21–8 down in the Indoor International match against Scotland at Crystal Palace in 1960. The end illustrated in my diagram was the sixteenth.

With my wood to come, we were lying one shot, with Scotland's bowl behind the jack being second wood.

With Sid Martin, my third man, we deliberated what to do. I approached Ted Whitfield, who was our captain, at the end of

Plate 4. An example of a freely swinging left arm in delivery by Peter Line, twice England singles champion.

Plate 5. An example of left arm supported by left leg during delivery by Percy Baker, four times England singles champion.

Plate 6. George Warman Cyphers Denny Cup winning shot, March 1965.

Plate 7. A great indoors bowler, Arthur Knowling, at the Crystal Palace.

our rink explaining that if I made a mistake we would lose two shots, but if successful we could count a four.

As a result, I took a chance and rested the wood out to count the valuable four shots.

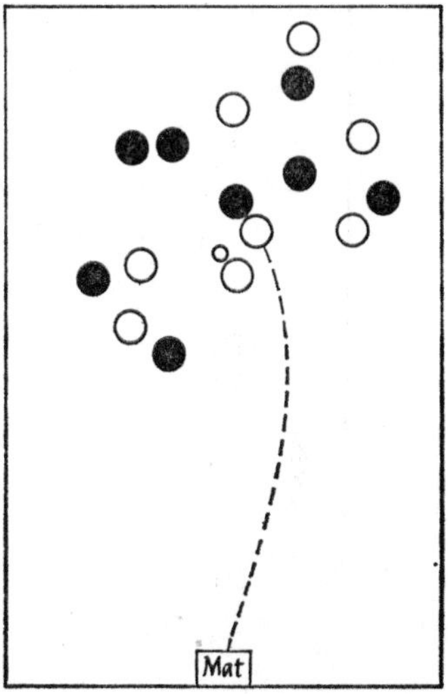

Fig. 31. England's bowls are white, Scotland's black.

This was the turn of the tide. With a running wood from Sid the next end, and with me to draw, we claimed another four shots and finished 24 to 22, two up after being 13 down. A most exciting finish to an international game.

Bill Tate, former British Isles singles champion

My greatest end was probably during the final against Scotland's Willie Adrain—not so much because of any dramatic or high-scoring swing, but because it showed Adrain my ability to bowl well under pressure and produce a telling shot when crisis threatened.

It happened on the tenth end when neither had been able to break away. I was leading 8–7. With my last wood, I faced the situation as shown in the diagram. Adrain had a good position and my front wood was dangerously close to the draw.

It was no use trying the forehand. My only hope was to get at him on the backhand but I was frightened of catching my own front wood. It was important to stop him scoring as we were very close to one another and any slight swing was probably going to have an effect on one or other of us.

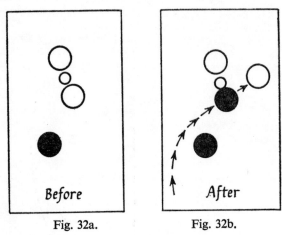

Fig. 32a.   Fig. 32b.

Adrain's bowls are white, Tate's black.

I took the backhand with 3 or 4 inches of run on it. I couldn't put much on because my wood had to come back a long way.

My wood just crept past the front wood, came round in a big draw, pushed him out and stayed right on the jack for the shot.

He never bowled quite so well again after that and it gave me confidence. I shall always remember that as the shot that swung the final.

9
Lessons of the 1970 Commonwealth Games

If you are like me, you normally watch bowls fairly intently but without making it a particularly exacting task. At the end of the match you will have a fairly sound idea of who bowled badly and well, where the crises arose, when the match took on any significant changes and so on.

Maybe there are rare occasions when you watch far more purposefully; perhaps you have been put on the club selection committee or you are trying to decide how best you and your friends might line up for the following year's county competitions. Maybe you have had a small bet on the outcome of a meeting.

In such circumstances you may well discover afterwards that many of your conceptions were not as accurate as you would have believed. For instance, consider the question I am about to put before reading beyond the end of this paragraph. In the last hundred pairs or fours matches you have watched how many times were the winners behind when the twenty-first end began? Five perhaps; or seven; ten, twelve even. Just try to recall.

This thought, and many others of special relevance to successful bowling, followed a research I completed into 65 of the fours matches and 81 of the pairs contests in the 1970 Commonwealth Games.

In the case of the fours not one team of the sixty-five winners was actually behind after twenty ends and only three were level.

In the pairs two winning couples began the twenty-first end behind and two more began it level. Thus 62 fours and 77 pairs played their final ends from winning positions.

The best recoveries, in terms of changing deficits into leads took place during the five to ten ends period of fours matches and between the tenth and fifteenth ends in pairs.

This surprised me considerably because the skips in these matches were reputedly the best in their respective countries; certainly two of them were World champions while several others were medallists in either the World or Commonwealth Games championships. Logically these men are capable of producing last bowls on twenty-four ends which swing the score by three or four shots. Yet they had 292 chances and, at most, succeeded twice only. What was the reason?

Many readers may develop their theories on this. However, one subjective factor which a few of us at Balgreen arrived at came from the success of Hong Kong in winning the fours gold medal. It lay in the way the skip used his early men, particularly the number two, to keep the head sufficiently open to leave the third man and skip room to manoeuvre. In the cases of the rival fours anxiety plus head building all too often left the skip with no room at all for pulling off swings or saves.

Closer study supports this theory. Of 231 ends they played in 11 matches they lost 99 and won 132 which is not a tremendous ratio of wins to losses. Of the 132 they won 58 yielded singles. During the week they lost only one match. So, without further figures, it is abundantly clear that (a) they scored significantly more freely than their various opponents and (b) they were able to hold down the rate of opposition scoring. In fact, of that 99 ends lost 59 were singles.

My immediate feeling when faced with these facts are of doubt concerning traditional approaches to fours play. They brought back to my mind an incident when the lead in a four opposing Canada delivered a dead toucher with his very first bowl.

Without a moment's hesitation the opposing skip called on his lead to fire and this he did with such force and accuracy that the 'head' was killed, necessitating a replay. It is the only time in sixteen years of careful watching that I have seen an end killed by the second bowl delivered. The incident was scorned from the bank. Against England the Canadians killed no fewer than fourteen ends, leading one exasperated England team member to snort: 'That wasn't bowls, it was skittles.'

I am not advocating a sudden surfeit of firing, merely suggesting that the irrefutable figures arising from my research warrant one or two of our more thoughtful bowlers carrying out a series of wild experiments during 'friendlies'! They might discover tactics which will revolutionize fours play . . . and pairs, too.

The Hong Kong approach of an aggressive number two is in line with the attitude taken by John Scadgell when skipping England to the fours gold medal in the 1958 Empire and Commonwealth Games. Scadgell had as his lead Norman King, winner of a gold medal in the 1970 pairs. In the final play-off against South Africa it was fair to assume that King would, at least, have a level battle with the opposing lead. Indeed, had he used short jack tactics, he would probably have proved superior. But in fours play the leads deliver two bowls each, leaving the following six players with a further two per man—twelve in all. These can cause quite a clutter at the head.

Scadgell considered that on long jack play he was significantly superior to the South African skip. So, instead of allowing King to seek advantageous heads as lead and, perhaps, to close them up in consequence, he sacrificed King by calling for long jacks.

King had a moderate match only but Scadgell's confidence was amply justified for, with space in which to manoeuvre, he outbowled the South African skip and England won the gold medal. King, incidentally, was the man who revealed—and praised—Scadgell's tactics.

Scadgell is an adventurous bowler who frequently figures in

surprise results. Bob Stenhouse, England fours skip at the 1970 Games, is more orthodox and on the slow greens at Balgreen paid the penalty. Repeatedly he went to the mat pacing congested heads and, with the slow green severely restricting the use of 'land', this restriction of manoeuvring space was a severe handicap. As so often happens in such cases, fortune seemed to frown on him and England finished in a lowly position that was a travesty of their real standing.

Analysis of 65 Winning Fours at the 1970 Commonwealth Games

Progress

Ends	Winning	Level	Behind
5	38	5	22
10	52	4	9
15	54	3	8
19	59	4	2
20	62	3	0

Biggest swings

| | Ends | | |
	5–21	10–21	15–21
Gain in shots	27	20	13
Loss in shots	12	12	8

Overall change for 65 four winners

B = better   W = worse   N/C = no change

5–10 ends	B 45	N/C 6	W 14
10–15 ends	B 39	N/C 7	W 22
15–19 ends	B 44	N/C 4	W 17
19–20 ends	B 44	—	W 21

Of 22 behind at 5 ends, 18 improved position and 4 fell further behind by 10 ends.

Of 9 behind at 10 ends, 5 improved, 2 showed no change and 2 fell farther behind by 15 ends.

All the 8 who were behind at 15 ends improved their position by 19 ends.

Analysis of 81 winners in the pairs

Ends	Lead	Level	Behind
5	52	10	19
10	57	4	20
15	67	2	12
19	71	5	5
20	77	2	2

10

Personality and Champions

No matter how skilled your techniques and subtle your tactics, you still need a great deal more: perhaps 75 per cent of your full quota of assets, if you are to become a champion.

Firstly, you must be a good competitor. It is so easy to deliver bowl after bowl on the proverbial sixpence in practice or when playing someone far below yourself in a practice roll up. It's even easy, relatively, to bowl one's best against a man far superior in standard for in none of those situations are you under any damaging pressure.

Practice doesn't matter and in the other cases only something very unusual can cause you defeat or bring you victory.

So, to define a good competitor, he is a man who tends to bring out his best performances on a number of critical occasions, not where he is winning easily but where the occasion is big and the going tough.

Like the good sailor, soldier or airman, a good competitor feels subconsciously many of the pressures of war and so he must abound in controlled aggressive spirit, dominance and self-confidence.

These qualities are needed as much in preparation as in competition itself, for it needs considerable self discipline to work through demanding practice sessions without the stimulation or atmosphere of a crowd.

Incidentally, the Russians are very aware of this and now it is customary for parents, relations and friends to be encouraged to attend training sessions.

Motivation is important here, but not all important. There is in the animal kingdom a natural 'pecking order', as anyone who has seriously watched hens and other animals feeding will see. As if obeying some instructions beyond human hearing, they line up in a special order to wait their turn to feed.

And who is to say this does not apply to human beings? Who among us does not know a man who always gets served first in a pub or shop, or who always gets the only vacant table in a restaurant or who grabs the taxi we've been waiting for patiently for ten minutes?

So in games there are natural winners and routine losers. Skill scarcely seems to enter into it. One is a born winner, the other is a born loser.

However, humans have one great power missing in animals, namely reflection.

An animal knows how to perform many functions.

So does a man, but above that, he knows that he knows and so can move outside the problem and thus change it. He has the power to shape his own destiny.

This applies in bowls. Some men are naturally assertive, others are not. War time experience showed how difficult it is to change the latter. So why try unduly in sport? If you are normally submissive you will waste undue nervous and mental energy trying to become dominant.

Far better to accept this and concentrate your efforts on becoming more skilled technically and tactically. Skills tend to break down under pressure but if you are better practised than ever and expect pressure to be applied, your knowledge will enable you to withstand the pressure. Win a match or two and your confidence will grow. Win a few more and you will start relishing hard matches and from that moment on you will be on the home stretch.

Success is important but defeats are valuable. They must be used positively. The question, 'Why did he beat me?' must be

137

examined minutely and answered with scrupulous truth. Then the weaknesses which led to defeat can be discovered and rectified.

In match play positive, aggressive play tends to build confidence more than thoughtful accuracy. This, of course, means within reason—and when opponents are similar in standard.

When there is a wide disparity such factors are, on average, unlikely to affect the overall result though a sound mental approach can have a significant effect on the score.

David McClelland, a Professor of Psychology at Harvard University, has isolated a personality factor which he has named 'The self-motivated urge to achieve', symbolized 'N.ach'. It means that some men are so made that, irrespective of reward, they have to do anything they take on as well as they possibly can.

It may be building a jet plane or sweeping a road. It doesn't matter. They can only do it as well as possible.

Normally they are not particularly happy people but they do get things done. Even in America, where one thinks of an entire nation of 'go-getters', the proportion of 'N.ach' high scores is very low—possibly not more than one in a hundred.

Yet it is necessary in a champion—unless one can find a different motivation. This can be sheer enjoyment.

In life people occupy varying positions along the continuum which stretches from 'natural killer' to 'nice guy'. So where do you stand?

If you are a 'killer' you are likely to be highly motivated for winning. May be you will also be naturally skilled and persistently industrious, in which case you will be unique among millions and your results will equal those of David Bryant.

More practically, your sheer determination to win will enable you to overcome bowlers whose technical skills are superior to your own. Putting it in figures your talent may be, say, 60 but your concentration and tenacity are 100 per cent. Then your effectiveness will be 60.

138

Compare this with someone who has 90 for talent but is only 50 per cent efficient. His effective score is only 45. In planning and practising for improvement think both of technical skills and temperamental determination. All can be developed but only through intense effort.

Nevertheless, you will play many matches in which you will feel your opponent has more determination to win than you. Perhaps you can key yourself up to better him in a battle of wills but my belief is that positive action to play better bowls is a superior attitude.

Put practically, this means that whenever you find yourself under pressure, you turn your efforts positively to attempting simply to deliver your bowl with the smoothest, technically best style of which you are capable.

Before beginning your delivery, you stand on the mat and imagine not only this near perfect delivery but also the actual course of your bowl as it travels down the green and curls in to take its objective.

Imagine this so strongly and vividly that you can feel it in the very marrow of your bones. Then, indeed, your mind will be positively and exclusively concentrated on your own objectives that it will be impervious to the ploys or mental pressures being applied by your opponent.

He may still win but you will know this to be on merit. There is no parallel to this in games where the opponent has a direct effect on what you do. For example, in cricket his leg break may be more heavily spun, or better disguised, or faster, or. . . ? In each case your shot is governed directly by the ball as projected by him to you.

Similarly, in tennis, he may hit the ball harder, or nearer the lines, or with more spin, or . . . ? than anyone you have played before. Thus he can bolster any psychological advantage with a technical superiority which may destroy your skills.

In bowls, as in golf, he cannot do this. He can attack the head, block it; build it to perfection and so on but when you step on the mat you are in sole possession of the rink. You may stand on

139

it where you will and can take just as long as is sportingly fair before you actually deliver your bowl.

The mat has an area in excess of 300 square inches so it offers tremendous scope for variation. When David Bryant beat Geoff Kelly in the 1970 Commonwealth Games a combination of Kelly's skill, will to win and a tricky green had Bryant in difficulties until he saw that Kelly was bowling on the forehand from the backhand side of the mat so he adopted this himself and from then on suffered no more major problems. He used his opponent's tactical skill to overcome a scoring and, to some extent, psychological superiority.

When you are able to summon up the technical strength of a Bryant you, too, will be able to counter determination with better bowling supported by a concentration unaffected by anything fair the opponent may do. And the umpire is there should he attempt anything unfair.

Bill Tate showed this ability when winning the British Isles Singles Championship in 1963 against Willie Adrain. Noticing he never watched Adrain's bowl but simply looked at the head after it had come to rest, I asked him why. He answered, 'Why should I get myself worked up over what his bowl might do? I can't stop it so I just look at the head after it has stopped and save all my mental energy for my own play.'

That happened in singles but what of fours play? Wartime research into the performance of R.A.F. bomber crews produced considerable information, some of which is relevant to bowls.

Primarily I am concerned with effects with one or more members of a unit out of form; when everyone is bowling well troubles seldom arise.

The object at such times is for the other members of the four not to lose their form while either helping the off-form member to find his usual form or, if he is having one of those really stinking days which beset us all from time to time, to carry him as much as possible.

Two factors must be considered, the first that no man bowls

140

badly on purpose, the second, that if he is off form he is likely to feel far worse about it than his team mates—providing he continues quietly to try as hard as he can without lapsing into self pity or moaning. If he labours the point of his poor form, is unduly apologetic or tries to make excuses and so on, his attitude will slowly but surely bring down the rest of the four.

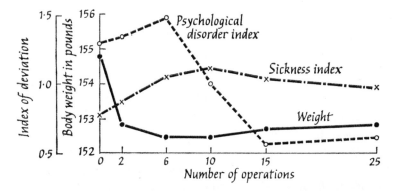

Fig. 33. Wartime reaction of R.A.F. bomber crews as number of operations increased. This suggests that too much competitive bowling is likely to spoil performance. It is better to mix competition and practice.

So to the man who is suffering a bad day, my advice is keep quiet, try as hard as you can, take your time, make a determined effort to use the mental rehearsal routine covered earlier in this book and consciously relax your shoulder and arm during your actual delivery.

To his team members I suggest completely natural behaviour. Neither overdo nor underdo sympathy or advice but be ready to offer any really practical tip. For example, poor form normally leads to over anxiety and over anxiety in all games leads to one very common fault.

It is looking up during the actual moment of action to see where the ball has been hit, picked, thrown or delivered. The other common faults are hurrying and pressing.

So a wise skip will first try a few practical tips—suggest the land to take, for example. If this doesn't work a quiet 'take your time, keep your head down and relax' may well work wonders for in such situations sports players need positive thoughts to cling to.

Very occasionally a man may need driving—bullying even—but ninety-nine times out of a hundred he requires positive thinking and confidence building.

Can a top class bowler's personality, a more all embracing term than the normal word character, be analysed in any kind of detail?

The short answer is 'yes' because personality measurement is now commonplace in games like football and tennis while in industry many giant international organizations would not dream of hiring an executive without taking precise account of his basic personality structure.

So far as tennis is concerned, *Lawn Tennis*, the sister magazine of *World Bowls*, has provided the definitive work on players, but work has only just begun on bowlers.

Fundamentally, one should, perhaps, hypothesize an ideal bowls personality and then relate it to those revealed by investigation of world class players.

There are two world authorities on measurement of personality, Professor H. J. Eysenck of the Maudsley Hospital, Dulwich, London, and Raymond B. Cattell, an Englishman professionally engaged at the Institute.

There are slight differences of approach between these two giants in the world of psychology and for reasons which need not be discussed here, my work has all been done using the Cattell method.

This isolates sixteen separate facets of personality and then, through a scientific questionnaire validated by millions of tests, measures the strengths of these in the individual under test.

Some of these factors are of great importance in bowls, others less so. Some can be grouped together to show anxiety quotient (high is bad for nervous games players) and extraversion/intro-

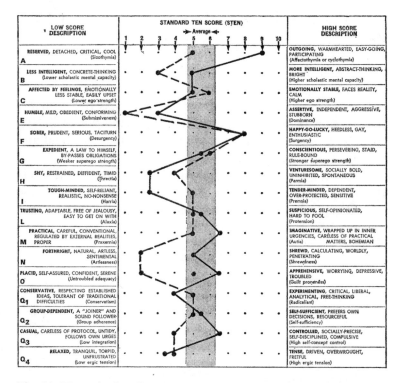

LOW SCORE DESCRIPTION	STANDARD TEN SCORE (STEN) ➤ Average ◀	HIGH SCORE DESCRIPTION
A	RESERVED, DETACHED, CRITICAL, COOL (Sizothymia)	OUTGOING, WARMHEARTED, EASY-GOING, PARTICIPATING (Affectothymia or cyclothymia)
B	LESS INTELLIGENT, CONCRETE-THINKING (Lower scholastic mental capacity)	MORE INTELLIGENT, ABSTRACT-THINKING, BRIGHT (Higher scholastic mental capacity)
C	AFFECTED BY FEELINGS, EMOTIONALLY LESS STABLE, EASILY UPSET (Lower ego strength)	EMOTIONALLY STABLE, FACES REALITY, CALM (Higher ego strength)
E	HUMBLE, MILD, OBEDIENT, CONFORMING (Submissiveness)	ASSERTIVE, INDEPENDENT, AGGRESSIVE, STUBBORN (Dominance)
F	SOBER, PRUDENT, SERIOUS, TACITURN (Desurgency)	HAPPY-GO-LUCKY, HEEDLESS, GAY, ENTHUSIASTIC (Surgency)
G	EXPEDIENT, A LAW TO HIMSELF, BY-PASSES OBLIGATIONS (Weaker superego strength)	CONSCIENTIOUS, PERSEVERING, STAID, RULE-BOUND (Stronger superego strength)
H	SHY, RESTRAINED, DIFFIDENT, TIMID (Threctia)	VENTURESOME, SOCIALLY BOLD, UNINHIBITED, SPONTANEOUS (Parmia)
I	TOUGH-MINDED, SELF-RELIANT, REALISTIC, NO-NONSENSE (Harria)	TENDER-MINDED, DEPENDENT, OVER-PROTECTED, SENSITIVE (Premsia)
L	TRUSTING, ADAPTABLE, FREE OF JEALOUSY, EASY TO GET ON WITH (Alaxia)	SUSPICIOUS, SELF-OPINIONATED, HARD TO FOOL (Protension)
M	PRACTICAL, CAREFUL, CONVENTIONAL, REGULATED BY EXTERNAL REALITIES, PROPER (Praxernia)	IMAGINATIVE, WRAPPED UP IN INNER URGENCIES, CARELESS OF PRACTICAL MATTERS, BOHEMIAN (Autia)
N	FORTHRIGHT, NATURAL, ARTLESS, SENTIMENTAL (Artlessness)	SHREWD, CALCULATING, WORLDLY, PENETRATING (Shrewdness)
O	PLACID, SELF-ASSURED, CONFIDENT, SERENE (Untroubled adequacy)	APPREHENSIVE, WORRYING, DEPRESSIVE, TROUBLED (Guilt proneness)
Q1	CONSERVATIVE, RESPECTING ESTABLISHED IDEAS, TOLERANT OF TRADITIONAL DIFFICULTIES (Conservatism)	EXPERIMENTING, CRITICAL, LIBERAL, ANALYTICAL, FREE-THINKING (Radicalism)
Q2	GROUP-DEPENDENT, A "JOINER" AND SOUND FOLLOWER (Group adherence)	SELF-SUFFICIENT, PREFERS OWN DECISIONS, RESOURCEFUL (Self-sufficiency)
Q3	CASUAL, CARELESS OF PROTOCOL, UNTIDY, FOLLOWS OWN URGES (Low integration)	CONTROLLED, SOCIALLY-PRECISE, SELF-DISCIPLINED, COMPULSIVE (High self-concept control)
Q4	RELAXED, TRANQUIL, TORPID, UNFRUSTRATED (Low ergic tension)	TENSE, DRIVEN, OVERWROUGHT, FRETFUL (High ergic tension)

Fig. 34. The unbroken line shows the personality make-up of one of the greatest gold medal bowlers in history. The broken line shows the personality of one of the all-time great, post World War II, Wimbledon tennis champions.

It shows that both are average in terms of realism (factor C) and in conscientiousness (G). They are more humble than average (H), indicating willingness to learn, and low in nervous tension (Q4). They are ultra low in factor O, showing self-confidence and serenity. The scorings on O and Q4 whow they are unusually well adapted to withstand the pressures of big occasions, one of the attributes of a champion. They are also strongly enthusiastic, suggesting that love of their games comes before thoughts of rewards, another important characteristic of true champions. Despite his warm nature (A) the bowler is outstandingly tough mentally. These personality measurements were made by *World Bowls* magazine, which has a highly skilled department for carrying out these and other analyses, which can assess a novice bowler's likelihood of progress, and the standards he is likely to attain.

143

version—introverts tend to be more persistent and better learners.

The answers are plotted on a chart and the result in respect of one gold medallist bowler of world fame is shown by the solid line on diagram 34.

If you are still reading, I believe you possess two valuable factors, namely interest and ambition. I hope this book will help to build another, namely pleasure in exercising your mind and will in trying to improve.

For, in the end, whether you be a bowls tiger or rabbit, surely the ultimate object is the human one of pleasure, in this case from accepting and meeting the challenge of seeking to become a champion, if only of your club.

11

How Champions Win

However profoundly one studies and understands the theories of bowls techniques, tactics and temperament, the ultimate test comes always in competition on the green.

It is therefore reasonable to assume that men who are chosen to represent their countries in international matches and championships must have attained some mastery of the theory—consciously or subconsciously—and then learned how to put it into effective action. I am thinking now of countries like England and Scotland where low-income bowlers are not, through cost, prevented from participating at such levels.

So it has been my procedure regularly to carry out researches into the play and ideas of men who attain this standard. In terms of number the biggest result from my research was in 1968, when it included no fewer than 43 internationals, a total which statistically assures a very high degree of validity in the findings. The 43 were:

1. P. Willis	2. A. Whitehead	3. W. E. Hart
4. J. A. Lewis	5. V. Oliver	6. C. S. Rew
7. S. E. Martin	8. F. I. Smith	9. A. F. Lewis
10. W. R. Edgar	11. G. Shooebridge	12. J. W. Heath
13. C. H. Woodhouse	14. P. Brimble	15. R. E. Lewis
16. T. F. Dimmack	17. A. A. Walter	18. J. Dominey
19. W. F. Taylor	20. E. A. Hayward	21. K. Freeman
22. L. G. Root	23. F. H. Thomas	24. J. G. Mann
25. G. S. Drake	26. H. Stevenson	27. R. C. Higgs
28. K. Andrews	29. A. Bates	30. T. B. Hamilton
31. C. Sweeting	32. J. W. Girdwood	33. C. O. Pearce

34. D. Swan	35. B. Maquire	36. R. Rowe
37. R. H. Stenhouse	38. J. A. C. Killick	39. S. Bond
40. G. H. Scadgell	41. H. Kneebone	42. T. H. Probert
43. A. Bennett		

The questionnaire contained 26 questions and, on analysis, the answers were extremely revealing. Here are a few.

Starting with grip, the breakdown showed that 11 use the cradle, 7 a finger grip, 11 the claw, 5 the thumb and 2 an open hand.

Before continuing, I should mention that the answers do not often total 43. Some were too indefinite to classify, others did not answer that particular question at all, and in some cases there were two or three different answers by one man to the same question.

The replies regarding delivery style showed more uniformity, 32 using the upright, athletic style; 5 a full-crouch and 5 a semi-crouch.

As was to be expected among such a rarified strata of bowlers, 33 expressed no preference for either hand, 5 nominated the forehand as favourite, 4 the backhand.

Surprisingly, perhaps, 18 do not vary the mat position a great deal and 10 do not vary jack length greatly.

Regarding mat position, 13 vary it a lot and 12 are affected by various considerations such as the green, opponent and so on; 17 vary the jack length a lot and 16 are governed by relevant factors on the day.

Bowls has become highly competitive, prizes well worth winning—the Teesside *Evening Gazette* gave a fortnight's foreign holiday for two as first prize for their 1972 'International Masters Tournament'—but, seemingly, even the majority of internationals regard the game as recreation because only 17 undertake special training or practice for bowls while 26 do nothing in particular.

With regard to the green, 22 prefer fast greens, 2 medium pace, 8 have no preference and 10 have varied likes and dislikes, depending on circumstances.

Recalling that 32 use the athletic delivery and 22 prefer fast greens where fine touch is vital, I would have expected more bowlers of this calibre to have worked on leg strength and control. After all, the athletic delivery is one of flowing movement. That movement must be effortless and rhythmic if control is to be constant. The key factor governing such a movement is stability and strength of leg for without it the rest of the body and the arms must inevitably jerk during delivery, in which case accuracy and consistency becomes a matter of luck rather than design.

What type of bowls do they use? The answers are 34 composition, 2 lignum, and 7 either composition or lignum.

Does an early start help? Seemingly not if international colours are your ambition. The ages when 43 men began playing were:

26	16	23	25	34	15	$17\frac{1}{2}$	30	42
47	31	32	37	13	11	48	42	45
43	35	25	28	40	24	25	33	37
36	29	35	40	32	29	45	15	60
10	18	19	14	32	47	13		

Anyone who wishes to check any individual bowler's starting age need only look up his number on the list on page 145 and then count that number of ages from the start.

The ages at which they played in their first competitions were:

26	19	24	26	34	16	18	30	44	48	31
33	37	15	19	49	43	47	43	36	26	30
41	20	38	34	39	37	29	35	41	36	30
45	17	61	23	23	29	38	33	48	16	

Other questions provided revealing and thought-provoking answers. For example:

Which is your best shot?

37 Draw Shot; 3 Fire Shot; 2 Rest Out; 3 Yard On; 2 Depends on Circumstances.

What is your favourite length?

1 Full Length; 6 Medium Length; 14 Three-quarter Length; 4 Short; 6 Depends on Circumstances.

Do you have any special tactical ideas?

17 No (a lot depending on opposition)   19 Yes

If so what are they?

3 Look for opponents' weaknesses and strengths.
1 Get opposing skip to fire.
1 Look for 8 shots an end.
2 Vary the mat and jack length.
2 Positional play.
1 See series of articles in *World Bowls*.
2 Keep game tight and get in front.

1 Get one wood at back of jack.
1 More than one wood in head.
1 Use better hand to get shots.
1 The heads must in all games be built to win maximum and lose minimum.
1 Adjust tactics as game proceeds —confidence.

Which is your most memorable match?

1. Playing for England in Belfast. — First International.
2. Playing against Scotland in Ireland. — First International—had to win.
3. Essex v. Middlesex. — Result depended on last shot.
4. 21–0 Win in National Championship. — Bryant's bowling and sportsmanship.
5. International at Boston, 1959. — Pulled back from 13–22 to 24–22, praise from Ogilvy.
6. First International. — Realization of ambition.
7. Quarter-Final in Gold Badge, 1964 singles. — 28 ends played—2¾ hours, 21–20.
8. First played for England. — Realization of ambition.
9. International v. Wales at Crystal Palace, 1961. — My best game ever.
10. England v. Scotland at Dundee. — Beat Stevenson's rink by 10 shots.
11. The last game played. — Analyse game after play ends, then forget.
12. Winning National Pairs, 1954. — Winning major honour at second attempt.
13. Winning Sussex Singles. — My third final.
14. 1964 International Outdoor at Belfast. — My rink broke international score against Wales.
15. Final of E.B.A. Singles, against — Too obvious to mention.

E. P. Baker, 1965, and v. R. Hitchcock, Sussex Final, 1965.

16. Championship cup.	Tight match 20-all, 2 inches from jack and drew shot without moving.
17. 1955 Middleton cup.	Badly wanted to win M/c Badge.
18. Final of Triples, against P. Baker (Mortlake), 1960.	Second highest honour to win National Competition.
19. British Isles Match.	Wonderful game.
20. E.B.A. Singles Semi-Final.	Cracking game, playing Bryant.
21. First International.	Playing for England.
22. Indoor Series, 1966.	First series as a skip.
23. Final E.B.A. Triples, 1952.	Won on merit.
24. Losing to Yorkshire in Middleton Cup Final.	Taught me never to count chickens.
25. Indoor International.	A bowler's ambition.
26. International Match at Desborough, 1968.	Playing against top bowlers.
27. North Acton v. Marion, Middlesex Cup.	Skipping and won on last end.
28. Semi-Final of E.B.A. Singles.	Fought back from poor score but lost.
29. Singles Final, 1967.	Bryant is World Champion.
30. There are many.	—
31. International Singles, 1966–7.	Whole England party really a team.
32. Against Wales, 1964 International.	Rinks won by a record score.
33. Many.	1964 International—because I played 3 rotten games.
34. Winning Surrey County Pairs as skip.	After being 13–1 down finished 11 up.
35. Indoor Singles, against Alan Bates.	Learnt more in 2 hours than in previous 2 years.
36. Final of National Singles.	—
37. E.B.A. Pairs Semi-Final, 1965, against Rhys-Jones and Bryant.	Because S. Carter and I brought the best out of Bryant.
38. E.B.A. Rink Final, 1937.	Excitement and good play.
39. Against Bryant in County Singles Final, 1962.	First major competition win.
40. —	—
41. Mortlake beat Hants, 1960.	—
42. First International in Belfast.	Honour of playing for country.
43. Weston Tournament.	Well run.

What is the best piece of advice you have been given?
1. Never underestimate your opponent.
2. As for 1.
3. To keep my eye on the rink.
4. Practise thoughtfully.
5. Practise.
6. Opponent has got same woods as you have.
7. Learn to lose.
8. Keep calm.
9. Keep to lead as long as possible.
10. Never fire with only one wood in the head.
11. Be honest with regard to one's own faults.
12. No substitute for match play.
13. Concentrate.
14. Be good sport and accept defeat.
15. 'Be happy on the green' (my wife).
16. Concentrate.
17. To lead for three years.
18. Never give in till last wood comes to rest.
19. Draw a length.
20. Never worry about games lost.
21. Take your time.
22. Ensure that one of your woods is nearest the jack.
23. Drawing is the game.
24. Always have at least second wood.
25. Be a good loser.
26. Concentrate.
27. Bowl a length wood.
28. The game is never lost until won.
29. Never play a match too soon after a meal.
30. To draw more than fire.
31. Making sure of mat position.
32. If you cannot get shot get the second shot.
33. —
34. Always respect your opponents' play.
35. Keep calm.

36. Try to bowl a length.
37. Regular and diligent practice.
38. Play naturally.
39. Drawing shot pays best dividend.
40. Take more time over first two woods.
41. To be able to lose as well as to win.
42. To use the draw 99½ per cent in singles.
43. Concentrate.

As a man who has played for his country what piece of advice
would you give to any average bowler who asked for it?
1. Don't let nerves beat you.
2. Practise.
3. Concentrate.
4. Concentrate.
5. Play your normal game.
6. Build the lead carefully and be ready for the unexpected.
7. Play as much as possible.
8. Concentrate on length and set progressive targets.
9. Concentrate.
10. 'Overgreen' rather than 'undergreen'.
11. Be honest regarding your faults.
12. Concentration.
13. Concentrate.
14. Play and be a good sport.
15. Enjoy the game you lose.
16. Be modest.
17. Lead for at least three years.
18. Keep trying and never be satisfied with second place.
19. Draw a length.
20. Be different—bowl the way you feel most comfortable.
21. Tournament play.
22. No hurrying after end completed, practise drawing.
23. Keep fit, keep sober and concentrate.
24. Enjoy your bowls.
25. Be a good loser.

26. Put up a bad wood, correct it on next one.
27. Try to bowl length woods.
28. Have some aim in mind and go for it.
29. Play to win.
30. To play No. 1.
31. Never try to play in all positions.
32. Take your green and never bowl short.
33. —
34. Be ambitious and learn laws of game.
35. Concentrate and be ready to learn.
36. Practise when you can.
37. Regular and diligent practice.
38. Concentrate on length.
39. Read the greens—concentrate.
40. Play competitive bowls as much as possible.
41. Give the player help—take him on green and iron out faults.
42. Enjoy the game, whether win or lose.
43. Learn to dead draw consistently.

Perhaps the most revealing answers related to the questions concerning nervousness, specifically in the first match each man played for England.

Altogether 25 admitted to nervousness while 18 did not. Ignoring the 18 for a moment, of the 25 all but one found this oppressive. Those who were able to locate effects answered:

Butterflies in the stomach 13, sweating 3, taut muscles 2, fast heartbeat 1, dry throat 1, variety of symptoms 5.

All recovered from nervousness fairly quickly, varying from the moment play began until 'five or six ends'. Just one bowler confessed to nerves for most of his first match.

The question, 'Have you found any way of overcoming nerves? If so, what?' produced some instructive answers, viz.:

1. Complete involvement in the game.
2. Confidence in ability.

6. Just relax.
7. Concentration.
8. Go into game in a positive frame of mind.
9. Depends on members of the rink you play with.
10. Taking one's time.
11. Maximum concentration.
14. After playing a few internationals you become used to it.
15. Concentration.
16. Steady breath and not bowling quickly.
17. No, but smoking helps.
18. Involvement in game.
20. By playing well.
21. Have a sweet.
22. Concentration and chewing.
24. No.
25. Play natural game.
26. Concentration.
27. Try to forget them.
28. Experience virtually eliminated nerve.
32. No.
34. By overcoming self-consciousness.
35. Concentration.
37. Once absorbed in game nerves disappeared.
39. Concentration.
40. Not to go on green too soon.
41. Become used to it.
42. Sit down when possible and relax.

If 43 England internationals may be called the 'cream of bowlers', then surely the men chosen to represent their countries in the 1970 Commonwealth Games at Balgreen, Edinburgh, may fairly be categorized 'cream of cream'.

They, plus one or two outstanding international and national championship winners, made up the 30 subjects of a second major investigation I carried out in July 1970. The full list of names is:

John Slight* (Scotland)
Aeron John* (Wales)
John Dobbie† (Australia)
J. Watson Black† (Scotland)
Denis Gosden* (Kenya)
Ernest Hodgson (Canada)
Sam Caffyn* (Canada)
William Scott* (Scotland)
Renato Motroni* (Scotland)
Alex McIntosh* (Scotland)
Alex Henderson* (Scotland)
William Tate† (Ireland)
Richard Williams† (Canada)
Norman Hook (England)
Thomas Jarvis* (Canada)

James Allison (Scotland)
Abdul Kitchell† (Hong Kong)
Osman Adem* (Hong Kong)
Clementi Delgado† (Hong Kong)
George Souza† (Hong Kong)
Geoff Kelly* (Australia)
David Hamblen* (Australia)
Frank Harrison (Australia)
Bob Purcell (Australia)
Charles Craig (Scotland)
Percy Jones* (New Zealand)
Gordon Jolly† (New Zealand)
Harry Reston* (Scotland)
Cliff Stroud (England)
Neil Bryce† (Zambia)

† Winner of gold or silver medal in World or Commonwealth Championships.
* Winner of national title(s).

The youngest anyone of these began bowling was 8, followed by 9, 10 and a couple at the age of 12. The oldest was 46 and the average size 32·10.

Ten were taught by their fathers, 6 by friends, 10 were self-taught and 1 by a professional coach.

Preferences were: singles 13, pairs 6, triples 1, fours 6, no preference 4.

Bowl sizes: $4\frac{7}{8}$ in., 1; $4\frac{15}{16}$ in., 1; 5 in., 11; $5\frac{1}{16}$ in., 10; $5\frac{3}{16}$ in., 1; $5\frac{1}{8}$ in, 5.

Grips: claw 13; cradle 6, finger-tip 6, pincer 1.

Deliveries: athletics 20, semi-crouch 2, crab 1.

Favourite positions: skip 16, third man 5, lead 8.

Their best bowls asset: draw shot 10; temperament 4, self-confidence 1, will to win 3; 18 admit to nervousness before and during big events, 12 do not.

Instructively, 15 believe this nervousness to be useful, 2 are neutral and only 1 thinks it harmful.

Now bowls as a game has yet to reach the same heights of publicity and money as tennis but it is, I think, instructive to read what Rod Laver, winner of over $500,000 in three years, had to say in a research on nervousness which I conducted among tennis players.

'I don't want to lose my nervousness as it makes me play well,' he answered. 'I keep moving my feet, talking to myself and just think about hitting the ball back.'

However, nervousness, even if it can be an asset by setting adrenalin flowing for action, has to be your tool and not your master. Can you conquer nerves? It depends largely on a personality factor called 'ego strength' and this was covered by my *World Bowls* report which read:

'Is nervousness prevalent in top class bowling? If it is, do those who suffer from it find it an asset or a liability? Those were two thoughts behind an extensive research carried out by *World Bowls* during the 1970 Commonwealth Games at Balgreen, Edinburgh.

'Altogether 30 bowlers answered a revealing questionnaire covering a number of factors relevant to competitive bowls. As representatives of their countries they were deemed to be the leading players and, thus, pace setters in those countries.

'Of the 30 investigation subjects 18 admitted to nervousness in varying degrees before and during important matches. The other 12 answered "not nervous" although one of the 12—at least—is known throughout his country and by me to be exceptionally nervous. Those who know him assert that his nervousness is a positive benefit to his performance although it causes him considerable suffering. He is, incidentally, the holder of a World Championship gold medal.

'Of the 18 who admitted to nervousness, 15 asserted that this is a desirable state—provided it does not become uncontrollable.

'Specific answers were: Aeron John (Wales): Useful because it enables a better, more keyed up performance. Denis Gosden (Kenya): Both (nerves before and during play) are useful if controlled but harmful if allowed to progress to panic. This often distinguishes the good big event player from the others. Samuel Caffyn (Canada): If I don't have a few butterflies before a game

155

I don't play my best. William Tate (N. Ireland): Absolutely essential for me. I cannot bowl in top form unless I get slightly tensed up. Dick Williams (Canada): Useful. If you are nonchalant and lackadaisical, that is exactly how you will play . . . Without success. Harry Reston (Scotland): If I didn't have them (nerves) I wouldn't play my game.

'A similar research carried out among top class tennis stars revealed that 32 out of 33 international champions suffer from nervousness and that four who are household names—Rod Laver, Margaret Court, Billie-Jean King and Tony Roche— have to be nervous to hit Wimbledon winning form. Why, though, should the ratio, 32 out of 33, be so much higher in tennis than in bowls, 18 out of 30?

'Some of the bowlers answered that they used to be nervous but, with age and experience, the tendency had vanished. Undoubtedly increasing age normally brings increased mental stability and a more philosophical attitude to life and this lines up with the findings of an earlier research which I carried out into the personalities—a more all-embracing term than character— of world class and international tennis players.

'The particularly relevant passages in the published paper reads; "However, on two primary factors the groups (World 'top-twenty' rankers and very good tournament players) were very different. The discriminating factors were F (Surgency-uncontrolled elation) and Q4 (Tenseness) in which the tournament players were significantly higher.

' "High surgency is very common among track and field athletes but it seems that first class players (tennis) need to be nearer the general population mean.

' "The high Q4 scoring of the tournament players would indicate that many of these players have not developed the ego-strength necessary to cope with the energy excitement generated in the game".

'Elsewhere the article reads. "Apparently for success in tennis a little basic temperamental anxiety may be useful so long as it can be controlled by compensating personality traits".

156

'Of these ego strength appears the most important. In the Handbook for the "Sixteen Personality Factors Questionnaire" by Raymond B. Cattell, Ph.D., D.Sc., and Herbert W. Eber, Ph.D.—Institute for Personality and Ability Testing, Illinois—the factors indicative of ego strength are listed: "Emotionally mature and stable, calm, phlegmatic, realistic about life, absence of neurotic fatigue, placid."

'The other end of the continuum lists "lacking in frustration tolerance, changeable (in attitudes), showing general emotionality, evasive (on awkward issues and facing personal decisions), neurotically fatigued worrying".

'The factor is said to be approximately 80% hereditary and 20% due to environment but I hold research proof that some players have increased their ego strengths by as much as three standard deviations—a tremendous jump—over a five year period.

'Five years may seem a long time but it isn't really when a player is aiming for the top. It can be done but it demands strong and persistent mental effort.

'So if you are nervous, realize this can be an asset. The champions make it work for them. If you are to emulate them you too, must learn to harness your nervousness. How? Each man to his choice but think about ego-strength.

'The manifestations of ego-strength are subtle and not always easily identifiable. The following quiz will give you an approximate—repeat approximate—idea of your own rating. It is intended for guidance and must not be considered a final and definite assessment! On the other hand, the test is basically sound and the result should not be ignored.

'Since the quiz is intended to help bowlers, do not stupidly cheat yourself. Answer the questions as truthfully as you can by underlining the answer nearest to your feelings about yourself.

(1) I suffer somewhat from claustrophobia.
    (a) occasionally, (b) never, (c) rarely
(2) I find myself repeatedly worrying over trivialities.
    (a) yes, (b) occasionally, (c) never

157

(3) My parents are understanding when I have to make difficult decisions.
   (a) yes, (b) moderately, (c) no
(4) I would like to change my life for one which is less demanding.
   (a) yes, (b) not sure, (c) no
(5) The tones in which people say things hurt me more than the actual words they use.
   (a) true, (b) in between, (c) false
(6) I find habits comparatively easy to change.
   (a) yes, (b) no, (c) uncertain
(7) I find life in the 1970s full of frustrations and restrictions.
   (a) yes, (b) in between, (c) no
(8) The weather has little effect on my mood and performance.
   (a) yes, (b) no, (c) in between
Now turn to the key below:

EGO STRENGTH KEY

Question	Your Score
(1) a 0; b 2; c 1;	....
(2) a 0; b 1; c 2;	....
(3) a 2; b 1; c 0;	....
(4) a 1; b 2; c 0;	....
(5) a 0; b 1; c 2;	....
(6) a 2; b 0; c 1;	....
(7) a 0; b 1; c 2;	....
(8) a 2; b 0; c 1;	....

Total _____

YOUR ANALYSIS

Score 13 to 16. Your ego strength appears to be above average and you should be able, through application to master most situations—including nervousness in sporting competition.

Score 10 to 12. Average ego strength. You should meet no undue difficulty in dealing with anxiety situations in competition though if you are strong in mental drive you may suffer nervousness fairly frequently.

Score 0 to 10. Below average ego strength and therefore, you should be a little watchful. If you are a teenager this may be a condition of your age and you could grow out of it. But Heaven helps those who help themselves. Take stock. Do you sink into a dream world all too often. Do you frequently imagine yourself in imaginary conversations in which you rout the other person. Are you too busy being envious of others' success, or in finding alibis for your own shortcomings, to give 100 per cent effort to your own plans for improvement. Accept you cannot do better than your best—and then strive to make today's best better than yesterday's, to-

morrow's better than today's and so on. Tall oaks from little acorns grow
—and in that way nervousness can be harnessed for your good.'

That brings me nearly to the end. I have, I hope, shown that
techniques and tactics are important. Yet in the later chapters
there seems to be strong proof that these are only 25 per cent
of the story.

Success is much more dependent on mental and psychological
factors. On ambition, the urge to achieve for the sake of achievement itself, not for cash or glory. On a temperament which can
withstand pressures, which is strongly disciplined. On a willingness to practise purposefully when it might be more pleasant to
have a few social ends with friends.

Yet is that really more satisfying than sinking oneself so fully
in an objective that one's mind is freed from all other considerations?

Can one grasp happiness and say, 'At this moment I am very
happy?' Is it not more usual that having fulfilled a long-term
project one realizes how this has dwarfed all else and so looks
back thinking how enjoyable it all was.

Bowls is a great game but it shares a common factor with
others, namely it offers most satisfaction—frustration, too—
when one is giving one's all.

Then, irrespective of the arrival, the journey towards the goal
offers untold satisfactions.

Bibliography

Badminton Library, The, *Bowls* (Longmans, Green, 1890).

Bryant, D. J., *Bryant on Bowls* (Cassell, 1966).

Cattell, R. B., *The Scientific Analysis of Personality* (Penguin, 1965).

Cave, L. W., *Guide to Turf Culture* (Pelham Books, 1967).

Dawson, R. B., *Practical Lawn Craft* (Crosby, Lockwood & Son, 1939).

Dingley, Humphrey J., *Touchers and Rubs* (1893).

Esch, Harold W., *Lawn Bowling Handbook*.

Evans, A. T., *Competitive Bowls* (G. Bell & Sons).

Eysenck, H. J., *Fact and Fiction in Psychology* (Penguin, 1965).

Fisher, John W., *World Bowls* (Normal Press, 1956).

Jones, C. M., *The Watney Book of Bowls* (Queen Anne Press, 1967).

King, Norman, *Tackle Bowls This Way* (Stanley Paul, 1959).

Knapp, Barbara, *Skill in Sport* (Routledge, 1963).

Linney, E. J., *A History of the Game of Bowls* (T. Werner Laurie, 1933).

Soars, Frank, *The Modern Approach to Bowls* (Wolfe Publishing).

Strutt, Joseph, *The Sports and Pastimes of the People of England* (Methuen, 1801).

Sweeney, Arthur, *Indoor Bowls* (Nicholas Kaye, 1966).

Whiting, H. T. A., *Acquiring Ball Skill* (G. Bell & Sons, 1969).